CONTENTS

ABOUT THE AUTHOR:

Betty Andrews is an author, spiritual teacher and motivational speaker. She's also the founder of Woo Woo, a global business that's all about spirituality and well-being.

Betty's is on a mission to raise consciousness and help people feel amazing about themselves and their place in the world. She's all about empowering people to pursue their dreams and live their best lives. And making it fun, and doing it in glitter.

Book Betty for coaching and speaking opportunities on www.bettyandrews.co

INTRODUCTION

When I decided to write this book, I didn't know it was gonna be a book tbh. I was making a whole bunch of blog posts on my personal spiritual journey and story. I hadn't really heard stories like mine and I certainly didn't have a lot of people to talk to about it. But the more I wrote? The more I saw that it was VERY clearly more than just a few blog posts. And I always knew I was gonna write a book, but I certainly didn't think it was about spirituality. I always thought I was going to write an epic sci-fi series of books, I didn't know that my life was actually gonna turn into what I used to think was fiction. And the title of this book? That's what I asked daily. WHAT THE EFF IS HAPPENING TO ME? AND WHO DO I SPEAK TO ABOUT IT? Because it was like being on hallucinogenic drugs. Except I very much wasn't and I kinda wish I very much was (when I was going through it). Because it was weird and hard and WEIRD.

Seeing spirits? Healing trauma? Losing friends? Knowing things psychically? Using universal life energy to heal? Removing entity attachments? SEEING ALIENS? Are you kidding me?

I had no freakin' idea what was about to happen to me. I also didn't know how to deal with it or who to speak to about it.

And eventually, I found those people and I found healers who changed my life. I found guides who helped me find and align with my purpose.

So, I wanted to write this for others who feel like they've

taken acid, find healing their trauma overwhelming and feel Goddamn alone.

I get that. I get you.

I'm writing this book for the wild ones. The witchy ones. The ones who've doubted their power. Who doubted themselves.

Through my own journey of self-discovery, I found that spirituality was the key to unlocking my true power and potential. To healing things I never thought I could heal. I know firsthand how easy it is to fall prey to society's expectations and lose sight of who we truly are. That's why my book is so important; it serves as a roadmap for women to come back to themselves and step confidently into their power. My hope is that every woman who reads it will find the same sense of liberation and strength that I did. It's time for us to break free from societal norms and live life on our own terms, and I truly believe that embracing spirituality is the way to do it. And it saved my life, honestly. I want that for you too.

We've been conditioned to fear each other since the dawn of time. The witch wound, the persecution, the constant messaging that we're not good enough, it's all designed to keep us small and powerless. But guess what? We're done with that nonsense. My book is here to show you how to step into your full power and heal yourself. It's time to break free from the chains of fear and embrace the magic that's been inside you all along. You don't need anyone's permission to be a badass; you just need to believe in yourself. So let's banish those old wounds and rise up together because when we support each other, there's nothing we can't accomplish.

There may come a time when disaster strikes in your life and it causes you to question EVERYTHING, and you can't explain it away. Suddenly, the whole damn meaning of your life goes up in smoke. It's a dark and scary place. This is when awakening happens.

Believe it or not, this could be your chance to transform into a badass, enlightened version of yourself. Your life will have meaning again, but it won't be something you can explain with the same concept of life that you've used before. Nope, quite often it's in this dark place that people wake up and realise that the old reality they thought they knew has gone up in flames.

When someone goes through the dark night of the soul, they come out the other side with something deeper, something more meaningful than they ever thought possible. They start to feel connected to something greater than themselves, something that can't be explained with some boring concept.

It's like a re-birth, baby! The old egoic sense of self dies, and a new, badass true self emerges from the ashes. Yeah, death is painful, but let's be real, nothing real has actually died. It's just that fake, illusory identity that's gone for good.

And get this, some people realise that going through this transformation was the key to their spiritual awakening. It's all part of the process. The death of the old self is just the beginning of the journey to becoming your best self. So, embrace that dark night of the soul, and get ready to rise from the ashes like the badass phoenix you were always meant to be!

Spirituality and personal development are basically two sides of the same coin. At their core, both spirituality and personal development are about becoming the best damn version of yourself. They're about getting to know yourself, your strengths, your weaknesses, and your purpose in life. They're about learning to love yourself and others unconditionally, and about finding your place in the world. So if you're thinking that spirituality is all incense and chanting, think again. It's about becoming the person you were always meant to be. And let me tell you, there's nothing more badass than that. But it is hard and it hurts too. Let's not deny that.

More and more individuals are tapping into their Divine gifts as they deepen their faith and embrace the higher awareness and consciousness of the 5th Dimension. Healing is happening rapidly and more often. The energies are in flux, and it's clear that 2012 was not the end of the world as some believed, but the start of a grand Awakening. So, don't be afraid to embrace the unknown and let go of that tired old way of thinking. It's time to transform into the badass version of yourself that you were always meant to be.

In my opinion, it seems like more and more people are reaching a point where they're ready for their own Ascension. Some folks have a major Awakening after recovering from a serious illness or having a profound spiritual experience. Others have already ascended and are showcasing their supernatural abilities in positive ways. It's all part of a shift into a new energetic alignment and a 5th Dimensional level of consciousness where love and joy reign.

So in an awakening, there comes a point when everything you thought you knew goes out the window. The meaning you gave to things based on society's conditioning and culture suddenly becomes meaningless. It's like you're living in a state of ignorance, and everything you thought you knew is gone.

But get this, it's actually a good thing! Without a mind-made framework of meaning, you can look at the world with fresh, innocent eyes. Sure, it might seem scary at first, but trust me, it's all part of the journey.

In fact, it's during this "dark night of the soul" that you truly start to see the world in a whole new light. You're no longer trying to fit your experience into some boring old conceptual framework. Instead, you're able to experience the aliveness of everything around you through your own sense of being.

So don't be afraid to let go of those old, tired concepts and embrace the beauty of the present moment.

Are you ready to awaken to your true self? Then this book is for you. In these pages, you'll learn everything you need to know about what a spiritual awakening is and what you can expect to go through when you have one. Trust me, it's not all rainbows and unicorns. You'll be questioning everything you thought you knew about the world and yourself, but fear not, because I'm here to guide you through it all.

But let's be real, the dark night of the soul can be a real b*tch. That's why my book will teach you how to handle it. And you don't have to handle it alone. You'll learn how to navigate the darkness and come out the other side stronger than ever. And yeah, you might lose a few friends and relationships along the way, but don't worry, because you'll be making room for the ones who truly align with your newfound self.

And let me tell you, questioning reality is where the real magic happens. In my book, you'll learn how to trust your intuition and tap into the power of manifestation. You'll discover the resources you need to call upon to heal yourself and align with your true self. You'll learn how to let go of the past and step into your full power, ready to take on the world.

So if you're ready to awaken your inner badass and take your life to the next level, this book is for you. It's time to stop living small and start living the life you were always meant to live. Are you ready to dive in and discover your true potential? Let's do this!

When you start talking about spiritual awakenings, people's eyes tend to glaze over like you're speaking a different language. But don't worry, because in my book, I'm speaking your language, baby. I know that a spiritual awakening can feel weird and confusing AF, but that's why I'm here to guide you through it all.

Let's be real, not everyone is going to understand what you're going through, but that's okay. You're not alone, and that's why this book exists. I'm here to hold your hand and help you navigate the ups and downs of this wild and crazy journey. Together, we'll explore the mysteries of the universe and discover the power that's been inside you all along.

So if you're feeling lost, confused, or just plain weird, trust me, I get it. But that's why my book is here to guide you through it all. We'll laugh, we'll cry, and we'll probably question our sanity a few times, but at the end of the day, we'll emerge stronger and more powerful than ever.

I wrote this book to share my personal journey and the things that have helped me. While I couldn't cover everything on the topic, I hope what I did include is useful to others. I plan to update the book with more information as I continue to learn and discover new helpful tips. If I can help at least one person, then I feel like my efforts are worthwhile.

CHAPTER 1: UNLOCKING YOUR INNER MAGIC: THE LOWDOWN ON SPIRITUAL AWAKENING

So let's start with what a spiritual awakening actually is shall we?

A spiritual awakening is like finally realising you've been sleepwalking through life and now you're wide awake! It's the moment when you understand there's more to existence than just what you see in front of you. It's realising you're connected to something greater than yourself and that you have the power to shape your life and reality.

When you go through this, it can feel like a wild ride. You may find yourself grappling with big questions like, "Who am I?" and "Why am I here?" Don't worry, this is all part of the journey. This process can be a little unnerving at first, but it's also filled with a sense of wonder and excitement.

We start realising that we've been identifying way too much with our egos. Because we are in fact, spirits having a human experience. And a part of waking up is this huge realisation. How much more there is to it all. We chose to incarnate here on earth, to be part of helping the world wake up, as well as to experience life on earth.

As conscious beings, we have the unique opportunity to experience the world around us in a way that no other species can. We are not simply physical bodies, but rather souls inhabiting human vessels. Our spiritual journey involves tuning into our soul and listening to its guidance, which often speaks to us through our intuition.

Learning to trust our intuition is a crucial step in our spiritual growth. Our intuition is our soul's way of communicating with us, guiding us towards our highest good and purpose. By learning to quiet the chatter of our mind and tune in to our inner voice, we can tap into the wisdom and guidance of our soul.

Our soul is the very essence of our being, and it is inherently oriented towards our well-being. It operates from a place of pure love, devoid of any fear or analytical judgment that often clouds our minds. When we listen to our soul, we can access a deeper level of understanding and clarity that is not limited by our physical senses or rational thinking.

As we journey through life, it's important to remember that we are more than just our physical bodies and our minds. We are eternal beings, connected to a greater consciousness that transcends time and space. By connecting with our soul and learning to trust our intuition, we can unlock the full potential of our spiritual journey and live a life of greater purpose, joy, and fulfillment.
Unlike the mind, which is susceptible to the influence of external factors and can be clouded by subjective beliefs, the soul has an innate ability to tap into a deeper understanding of our true nature and purpose. It serves as a guiding force that helps us navigate the complexities of life, making choices that align with our deepest desires and aspirations.

When we learn to tune in to the voice of our soul and heed its guidance, we open ourselves up to a world of possibilities that we may have never thought possible. We begin to see beyond the limitations of our mind, and instead embrace the infinite potential that lies within us.

In essence, the soul is our greatest ally in life, always working tirelessly in the background to steer us towards the best possible outcomes. It is a source of unwavering love, guidance, and support that we can always rely on, no matter what challenges we may face. By connecting with our soul, we open ourselves up to a world of limitless potential and endless possibilities.

An awakening is a profound realization that goes beyond the surface level of our everyday existence. It is the recognition that we are not just physical beings, but rather, we are souls inhabiting a human body, experiencing life in this physical plane.

This understanding is a powerful shift in consciousness that can transform our perception of ourselves and the world around us. It allows us to connect with the divine essence within us and realize that we are all interconnected in the vast universe.

A spiritual awakening is a deeply personal experience that can happen in many different ways. Some may experience it through a sudden revelation, while others may embark on a gradual path of self-discovery and spiritual growth.

Regardless of how it happens, a spiritual awakening often involves shedding old beliefs and attachments that no longer serve us, and embracing a new way of being that is aligned with our true essence. It is a process of letting go of the ego-driven mindset and embracing a more soul-centered way of living.

Through this process of awakening, we gain a newfound awareness and clarity of our purpose in life. We start to live with intention and take conscious actions that align with our soul's calling, rather than just going through the motions of life.

And we awaken to the truth of our environment. One of the bigger truths In my opinion being that the universe and everything within it is a simulated construct, created and controlled by higher dimensional beings. We have been convinced through our programming that we're in the world that we are in and it is in fact our thoughts creating the simulation. A lot of us are addicted to this game and reality we're creating, because of the relationships, situations and emotions which tie us to it. Which has convinced us it is real.

It sounds like science fiction, and for a long time afterwards, I still grappled with these concepts. My head is still trying to work my way around it. Because life really is more like *The Matrix* and *Star Wars* than I ever knew. But this is all part of what it means to wake up. Where you realise conspiracy, is more likely confirmation.

In a later chapter, I delve into the concept of reality and the matrix, which I believe you will find intriguing to explore. However, a crucial aspect of awakening is recognizing that our preconceived notions of reality may not be accurate, and realizing the immense power we hold in shaping the world around us.

Once you go through the awakening, you realise there are different levels of consciousness. Before it happens, you may have been on one of the lower levels of consciousness where the majority of the population operates. These levels are neither good nor bad, just simply a state of being. A lot of society is asleep. Operating within the paradigms of the system. Wake up, go to work. Come back. Watch the news. Believe the agendas. Outsource your power. Become eternally distracted. The purpose of what we're going through in an awakening is to understand the truth of it - that the power lies in us all along.

As you navigate this newfound territory, you may start to feel more in tune with your inner self. You'll begin to understand your thoughts and emotions in a new light and you'll gain a deeper understanding of the world around you. This shift in consciousness can lead to a greater sense of purpose, increased self-awareness, and a deep sense of peace and fulfillment.

You might feel like you've stumbled upon the secret to unlocking your full potential. It's like finding a hidden treasure within yourself! You'll start to feel more connected to your inner self and discover a deeper understanding of your thoughts, emotions, and motivations.

As you delve deeper into this connection, you may start to feel a newfound sense of peace and purpose. It's like finally figuring out the missing puzzle piece in your life. You'll start to understand why certain things happen and what your role is in the grand scheme of things. It doesn't happen straight away, and there are definitely a lot of ups and downs before it does. Although saying that, everyone's journey is very different.

One of the most exciting things about spiritual awakening is that it opens you up to new experiences and perspectives. You'll feel a greater appreciation for the world around you and a deeper connection to nature, people, and the universe as a whole. It's like seeing life through a brand-new lens and it's a truly amazing feeling.

So if you're feeling a little lost or disconnected, a spiritual awakening could be just what you need to get back on track. It's a journey of self-discovery that can lead to a greater sense of peace, fulfillment, and connection to the world around you. So go ahead, dive in, and see where this connection takes you!

Your awakening ain't just about realising what's going on in the world, it's about realising what's going on with yourself too. You gotta start questioning everything you thought you knew, and let me tell you, that's some scary stuff. I've been there, done that, and couldn't even talk to anybody about it. But don't you worry, this book is my gift to you. I'm here to help you make sense of all the nonsense and show you all the ways we can try. Trust me, I've been through it all in the past few years. Waking up to what I used to think was just my imagination - seeing spirits, talking to God, and even hearing the voices of trees. Like, seriously? That's the kinda stuff that gets you locked up. But guess what? It's all real, baby. And you can't convince anybody until they've been through it themselves.

Here are five signs that'll make it crystal clear you're going through an awakening.

1. You start questioning everything. The beliefs you've held your entire life suddenly don't make sense anymore. You might feel like you're living in The Matrix or something.
2. You become way more introspective. You spend a lot of time reflecting on your past, your present, and your future. You might even start a journal (or three) to help you work through all of your feelings.
3. You start experiencing synchronicities left and right. You keep seeing the same numbers (11:11, anyone?), you run into people who have the exact information you need, and you just generally feel like the universe is trying to tell you something.
4. You become super sensitive to other people's energy. You might feel drained after spending time with certain people, or you might feel like you're on top of the world after hanging out with others.
5. You feel a deep desire to connect with something greater than yourself. You might start meditating, practicing yoga, or going to church. Whatever it is, you just know that there's more to life than what meets the eye.

So, if you're experiencing any (or all) of these things, chances are you're going through a spiritual awakening.

If we're gonna start this story from the beginning, we gotta go way back to when I was just a lil' one. Like a lot of us who have gone through a spiritual awakening, I used to see spirits left and right. And let me tell you, I wasn't just seeing them - I could feel 'em too. They were all up in my face from every direction, and I even had some dark ones that stuck around for years. I remember being four years old and already having memories of seeing, hearing, and feeling those spirits. And like any other kid, I thought it was all in my head for the longest time. But oh no, what I experienced was so much more than just my imagination. See, my family lived in a house that was 5 to 600 years old, and my dad had fixed it up before I even came into this world. That should tell you something, right? In England, houses can date back centuries, and this one sure did. It looked beautiful, but let me tell you, it was also effing eerie.

Back in the day, I used to live in this old, creepy house that was haunted as hell. I'm talking spirits galore, but there was one in particular that liked to follow me around - even to the damn bathroom. I was so scared that I had to wake up my parents to escort me there. And let me tell you, it wasn't just seeing these ghosts, I could feel their damn hands on my legs at night. Needless to say, I still sleep in a cocoon of blankets to this day. I was so terrified of the dark that I taught myself how to lucid dream, so that at least I had some control over my consciousness. I didn't even realise what it was at the time, but hey, your brain does what it can to protect you. As I got older, the activity changed and these ghosts would take the form of things I was afraid of. It was like watching The Ring and then seeing that damn girl crawling after me on the stairs to the attic. I stopped watching horror movies in my 20s and 30s, but the ghosts still lingered. It wasn't until I went for energy healing that I realised something truly bone-chilling: it wasn't the house that was haunted, it was ME. I don't even know how the hell it happened, but I was carrying these ghosts with me for years. And let me tell you, burying my psychic and spiritual abilities was the only way to avoid daily horror. But now, here I am, ready to share my story with all of you.

My second awakening came knocking during the pandemic when I finally had to deal with the childhood trauma I had been dodging my whole life. So, I went on a mission to try every healing modality out there and stumbled upon energy healing. My Reiki healer, Kati Ackerman, dropped the bomb on me that I had an 'entity' attached to me. But let me tell you, I already knew about this entity for 24 years and it had been hanging around me like a bad smell. It was just nice to finally hear confirmation from someone else that I wasn't completely cray-cray. I mean, when you're going through a spiritual awakening, people will try and convince you that it's all in your head and that you're just a nutjob. And let's be real, not that long ago, people were committed to this kind of thing, and it's still happening today. So, I had to be careful about who I shared my truth with. The same entity had been with me all this time, but as I started working on clearing it, I had a huge breakthrough. This entity was attached to me through cords that went to my heart and my womb, and it was a malignant, parasitic energy that feasted on my energy. It was pretty intense and made me feel heavy, but I felt so much lighter when it was finally gone. Unfortunately, it came back after some time, even though I had been given prayers to keep it away. I think it was hard for it to let go of its attachment to me, after 24 years.

One day, I went to an acupuncturist who told me there was an entity attached to me. I didn't know this person at all, so it was wild that it was being confirmed to me. The acupuncturist did a ritual to remove the entity, and it worked! There was one day I saw a dark shape whilst watching TV, and it started coming towards me. But as it approached, it turned into a panther. It was a strange experience, but it made me realise that since we had healed the energy of the entity, it was no longer taking the form of my spirit guide. In fact, it introduced itself as Solomon, one of my main spirit guides now. This was a very profound and strange part of my journey, and it made me believe even more in spirit guides. Solomon often gives me advice, and I feel like he's been guiding me for a long time. Even as I write these words I'm like 'wtf'?!

It's like we're living in two different worlds - the regular one where we go about our daily business, and then the underground world where all these bizarre things are happening. And the worst part? You can't talk to anyone about it without being labeled as a nutjob. It's a lonely road, and it feels like you're the only one experiencing it.

It's like we were all those edgy teenage girls doing tarot cards and playing with Ouija boards, but then life happened, and we had to grow up and face 'reality.' But let's be real, sometimes we miss the excitement of those spooky games. But they're all real. Everything we believed in is real. And that's what this awakening is about. Realising that. And that's where the stress comes from because we're trying to align two very different realities.

Going through this can be a rollercoaster of emotions. Here are some of the feelings you may experience during this transformative time:

1. Confusion: As you start to question your beliefs and past experiences, it can be easy to feel lost and confused. This is normal, and it's all part of the process.
2. Awe: As you begin to see the world in a new light, you may feel a sense of awe and wonder. Everything may seem more vivid, and you'll have a greater appreciation for the beauty around you.
3. Excitement: Going through a spiritual awakening

can be a truly exhilarating experience. You'll feel like you're on a journey of self-discovery, and the possibilities are endless.

4. Emotional Release: During a spiritual awakening, you may confront past experiences or emotions that you've been avoiding. This can be overwhelming, but it's also a great opportunity to release any negative energy and feel a deeper sense of peace.

5. Transformation: The journey of a spiritual awakening can lead to a complete transformation of who you are and how you view the world. You may start to feel more confident, authentic, and aligned with your true self.

A spiritual awakening can be a mix of emotions, but ultimately, it leads to a greater sense of peace, fulfillment, and connection to the world around you. It's a beautiful journey of self-discovery but you might feel like you've been hit by a hurricane, 5 trucks and a flock of angry carnivorous seagulls tbh. BUT, it's a time to reconnect with who you are and what truly matters in life. So go ahead, embrace the unknown, and see where this journey takes you. You never know what amazing things may unfold!

How long does it last?

A Spiritual awakening isn't a one-size-fits-all experience with an expiration date. It's more like a journey, and you can never be sure where it's going to take you or how long it's going to last. Some people have a single, life-changing moment of enlightenment and are good to go, while others spend years or even decades exploring their spirituality and personal growth. It all depends on your own path and what you need to learn along the way. So, if you're looking for a timeline or an endpoint, you're barking up the wrong tree.

It's like waiting for your crush to text you back after a first date - you just don't know how long you're gonna be left hanging.

Spiritual awakening can be a wild ride, and not knowing when it's gonna end can be beyond frustrating. It's like you're on a rollercoaster and you can't see the end, so you just have to hold on and hope for the best. But that's much like life, eh? Life is full of uncertainties and a spiritual awakening is just one of them. Just a VERY weird one of them. You never know when it will start, how long it will last, or even what the outcome will be. But hey, that's just the nature of the beast, and you can't be attached to any of it. You gotta learn to let go of that need for control and just ride the wave.

I could go on and on about the benefits of letting go of control in a spiritual awakening! First off, it allows you to surrender to the universe and trust that everything is happening for your highest good. It also helps you release the need to constantly micromanage every aspect of your life, which can be a total energy drain. But I know what you're thinking: how the hell do you actually do it?

I am still learning this whole letting go of control thing myself. It's a constant practice, and some days are better than others. You're not going to be perfect at it, and that's okay. The spiritual journey is all about gradual growth and progress, not forcing everything to happen all at once. It's our ego that wants instant gratification and control, but that's not how spiritual awakening works.

So, if you're looking for some ways to start letting go of control, here are a few tips from someone who's still figuring it out:

1. Practice mindfulness: Being present in the moment can help you let go of the need to control everything that's happening around you. Focus on your breath and observe your thoughts without judgment.
2. Surrender to the universe: Trust that the universe has your back and everything is happening for a reason. Let go of the need to control every little detail of your life and allow things to unfold naturally.

3. Release attachments: Whether it's material possessions or relationships, letting go of attachments can help you let go of control. Remember that everything is temporary and detach yourself from the outcome.
4. Embrace uncertainty: Life is full of surprises, and not knowing what's going to happen can be scary. But, it can also be exciting and lead to new opportunities. Embrace the uncertainty and trust that things will work out in the end.
5. Practice self-compassion: Letting go of control can be a vulnerable and uncomfortable process. Be kind to yourself and remember that it's okay to make mistakes and take things one step at a time.
6. Find people to talk to: they're all over the interwebz. I have a community app called Woo Woo, where you can go find and meet other people going through this.

Is a spiritual awakening religious?

Spirituality and religion are like two siblings from the same family, but with completely different personalities. Religion is like that straight-laced sibling who follows all the rules, goes to church every Sunday, and reads from the same holy book. Spirituality, on the other hand, is the free-spirited sibling who explores their own beliefs, connects with the divine in their own way, and doesn't necessarily need a specific religious structure to do so.

Religion is more about adhering to a specific set of beliefs, practices, and rituals that are defined by an institution or community. Spirituality, on the other hand, is more about exploring your own inner world, finding your own path, and connecting with something greater than yourself in a personal way.

While religion can provide a sense of community and guidance, spirituality is more about individual growth and self-discovery. Religion tends to have more rules and dogma, while spirituality is more about personal experience and intuition.

Religion is like a boxed cake mix - everything is already laid out for you and you just have to follow the instructions. Spirituality, on the other hand, is like creating your own recipe from scratch - it might take some experimentation, but the end result is uniquely yours.

Spirituality is basically how we humans try to make sense of life and find our place in it. It's all about feeling connected to everything around us - ourselves, others, nature, and whatever we consider sacred or meaningful. And don't get it twisted, spirituality ain't the same as religion. It's not some set of rules or dogmas that you have to follow. It's more like a personal journey of self-discovery and growth.

Through this book, I'm going to help you see your spiritual awakening as the beginning of the rest of your life. Yes, it can be painful and there's a lot of healing to be done, but trust me, it's worth it. I've been through it and now I'm on the other side, living my best life.

CHAPTER 2: THE DARK NIGHT OF THE SOUL

Ah, the infamous "dark night of the soul" in a spiritual awakening. It's like that rude awakening you get when you realise that the spiritual path is not just about rainbows and unicorns. No, no, no! It's about confronting your demons, facing your fears, and slogging through the muck and mire of your own psyche.

The dark night of the soul is like a spiritual rite of passage, a gut-wrenching journey that can leave you feeling like you've been hit by a ton of bricks. You might feel lost, alone, and wondering if you've made a wrong turn somewhere.

A Spiritual awakening comes from confronting those fears, anger, guilt, and grief that have been holding you back. It's not about running away or trying to transcend those feelings, but rather coming to terms with them and using them as a launching pad for authentic spiritual growth. It's not always pretty or easy, but hey, nothing worth having ever is. The journey of spiritual awakening is often about much more than just experiencing new perspectives and feelings - it's also about healing. Here's why healing is such a big part of the process.

When you find yourself in the midst of a dark night, it's not just a matter of feeling down. In fact, it's loaded with symbolism that points to a deeper emotional level and possibly some memories that hold special significance. You have to keep your guard up, because hidden memories, stories, and worries can lurk beneath the surface. So, brace yourself, because there's a lot more to it than meets the eye.

A dark night of the soul is like a rite of passage, guiding you from one phase of your life to the next. It's a transformative experience that can occur more than once throughout your life, as you continue to evolve and become more fully immersed in the world around you. The ultimate goal is to emerge from each dark night stronger and more complete than before, with a greater understanding of yourself and your place in the world. So, embrace the darkness and trust that it will lead you to a brighter tomorrow.

One of the main reasons that I have my second spiritual awakening, was because like many people, I was in lockdown during the pandemic. I had no distractions and finally had to face the deal and heal my trauma. I've been diagnosed with PTSD and anxiety and depression. I managed all of these at a very high level, I was acting a lot of the time though. Infiltrating every part of my life, I found it really difficult to hold down full-time jobs because of overwhelm and a very highly strong nervous system, which made me too sensitive to virtually everything, to attracting the wrong relationships and friendships, because of a massive lack of self-worth. When you haven't been able to heal what happened to you, you will see the results of it in every area of your life.

It's crucial to survive the dark night, okay? So, face it head-on, give it a nod, take a good look at it and recognise its character. Yeah, let it hit you hard, but don't get too clingy or let it boss you around. You're not supposed to be the goddamn superhero who vanquishes the dragons and tries to completely obliterate the darkness. But, you gotta dig deep and find all the damn courage and determination you gotta get through it.

The first step to unlocking your full potential is to embrace the darkness. That's right, take that dark time and use compassion to guide you through it. It's not a nice experience, but it is needed to get you through to the other side. But, don't stop there. You need to sift through all the subtle innuendos of resistance and find those hidden images.

Those images may hold the key to your future success. It's all about turning that time into a journey, to emerge on the other side.

Don't even think about toning down the dark elements just because they're painful and discouraging. If you do that, you'll miss out on all the gifts waiting for you. Trust me, they're there. So, embrace that darkness, and get ready to unleash your inner badass.

I spent a long time trying to heal, but I think you just start to live with the pain and you think that it's normal but it's not normal. We're not supposed to live in pain and that's why after I started dealing with what happened to me, as a child and really accepted the two that I hadn't made it up, because I've been told that I made it up so that I come to believe that I was lying, which was even more traumatising. It's one thing to have something happen to you, it's quite another for you not to be believed. So I decided that I was gonna approach this, but I called the experiment. I was gonna try lots of different things because I was unwilling to end my life. I thought about it in so many ways over the years. And I just didn't want to think like that any more. I sometimes consult with brands on brand strategy and business strategy, you use data to understand the approach in which the business should take. Because opinions of one thing but data is quite another in business. And I thought what if I took this approach to my healing? What if I try things, and a series of experiments and see what the feedback and data were from my body and how I felt? And that's what I did. And that's what this chapter covers. Because

I can tell you now that I live without that trauma in my body. And for 30 years I never thought that that would be possible. It's an absolute miracle. And I was guided to think about the approach to healing in a way that made sense to my mind. Which was using experiments, data and feedback. And I truly believe that it was God/the universe that put them in there. The universe is always giving you ideas in a way that you will understand, you just have to listen to them and follow them, even if it seems a bit wild.

You don't just have to spend a fortune on therapy for years or live with the pain of your past. It's common to feel like doctors and therapists aren't helping, but that's not the only way to deal with physical, mental, or spiritual pain. But remember, I'm not a professional, I can only share MY experience. I lived with trauma for years and it almost broke me, but I found an amazing holistic therapist after searching for 17 years. Sure, society benefits from pain and the medical industry profits from it, but that doesn't mean it's the only solution. Holistic therapies may not be considered proper science in the Western world, but they've been used for centuries in Eastern cultures and they work because they address all parts of the body. Your mind isn't just in your brain, it's in your whole body, and if you don't deal with your pain, it can lead to dis-ease, which turns into DISEASE.

This book is about finding healing and coming back to yourself. It's a conscious choice to stop hurting and find peace. You don't have to suffer, and you don't have to be grateful for your trauma. Your soul may have chosen your path, but that doesn't mean it's easy. Beware of toxic positivity and narcissism in the spiritual world. We're all human, and we all struggle. This book is here to help you find healing and feel empowered, so you can help others too.

Depression and spiritual awakening may seem like two completely opposite experiences, but they can actually be closely intertwined.

On one hand, depression can be a catalyst for spiritual awakening as it often involves a deep sense of emotional pain, a loss of meaning or purpose, and a longing for something greater than oneself. This can lead individuals to question their beliefs and seek a deeper understanding of themselves and the world around them.

On the other hand, spiritual awakening can also trigger depression as it can be a difficult and challenging process. It may involve confronting painful emotions, letting go of old beliefs and patterns, and facing the unknown. This can be overwhelming and cause feelings of anxiety, sadness, and despair.

Depression is a mental health condition that can be characterised by persistent feelings of sadness, hopelessness, worthlessness, and a lack of interest or pleasure in activities. Depression can be caused by a combination of biological, environmental, and psychological factors, and there is no single spiritual cause or explanation for depression.

However, some spiritual teachers and practitioners believe that depression can be caused by a disconnection from one's true self or spiritual nature. This disconnection can be caused by a variety of factors, such as trauma, negative thought patterns, societal conditioning, and a lack of connection to a higher power or purpose. Further in the book, there is a whole chapter dedicated and coming back to yourself. Because that really is what awakening is all about. But you can't come back to yourself if you're not healing. Which is why this is such an important chapter.

In this view, depression can be seen as a spiritual crisis or a call to awaken to one's true self and purpose. Through spiritual practices such as meditation, prayer, mindfulness, and connecting with nature, one can begin to heal the root causes of depression and reconnect with their spiritual nature. It is important to note that while spiritual practices can be a helpful tool in managing depression, they should not be relied upon as the sole treatment for depression. It is important to seek professional help and support from mental health providers when experiencing symptoms of depression.

SHADOW WORK AND THE DARK NIGHT OF THE SOUL:

It's like everything you've built your life around just crumbles, and you're left feeling completely empty and depressed. Maybe someone close to you died, or maybe your life just took a nosedive for no apparent reason. Either way, you're left feeling like your entire existence is pointless.

It's like the rug has been pulled out from under you, and you're left spinning out of control. You question everything you've ever believed in, and wonder what the heck the point of it all is. It's a dark and lonely place, and it can feel like you're never going to find your way out.

But, the good news is that many people have experienced the "dark night of the soul" and have come out on the other side stronger and more resilient than ever. It's a tough journey, but if you're willing to face the darkness head-on, you may just come out the other side with a newfound sense of purpose and meaning.

During the dark night of the soul, everything you thought you knew about yourself and the world might come crashing down. You may be forced to confront your deepest fears, your most painful memories, and your most profound existential questions. It's like the ultimate identity crisis, where you're forced to reexamine your entire life and make sense of it all.

When you're going through a dark night of the soul, things can get pretty wild. It's like the universe is giving you a swift kick in the pants to wake you up and make you see things in a new light.

You might feel like your whole world is falling apart, and everything you thought you knew is suddenly up for grabs. It's a time of deep introspection and reflection, where you're forced to confront the parts of yourself that you might have been avoiding.

During this time, you might experience intense emotions like fear, grief, and despair. But it's not all doom and gloom – going through the dark night of the soul can also lead to a profound spiritual awakening and a renewed sense of purpose.

When you go through the dark night of the soul, you awaken into something deeper that can't be explained by any old concepts rattling around in your mind. It's like a total rebirth, where you ditch that egoic sense of self and connect with a greater life in a way that's not dependent on anything conceptual. Yeah, it might feel like a painful death, but let me tell you, nothing real actually dies there - it's just your illusion of identity that's kicking the bucket. And you know what? Some folks realise they had to go through that whole messy process just to achieve a spiritual awakening. So don't sweat it, babe - it's all part of the journey towards the birth of your true self.

So, while it might be a bumpy ride, just remember that the dark night of the soul is ultimately a necessary part of the journey towards enlightenment.

But here's the thing: the dark night of the soul is also a catalyst for transformation. It's a wake-up call that can shake you out of your complacency and push you to grow and evolve. It's a chance to shed old beliefs and patterns that no longer serve you and make way for new insights and revelations.

Confronting Past Trauma: As you begin to explore your inner self and question your beliefs, you may encounter past experiences or emotions that you've been avoiding. Confronting these feelings can be difficult, but it's also a great opportunity to heal from any past traumas or negative experiences. The process of healing trauma can also be called shadow work. Shadow work is a term used in psychology and spirituality to describe the process of exploring and integrating the darker aspects of our personalities, often referred to as the "shadow self." This shadow self is comprised of unconscious thoughts, feelings, and behaviours that we have repressed and disowned due to societal or personal values and beliefs.

When life throws us a curveball and we're faced with something too big to handle, our bodies go into survival mode. Whether it's a huge tragedy like a loved one's death, a car crash, or a natural disaster, or something a bit more subtle like neglect, abuse, or bullying, our minds will do what it takes to protect us.

Sometimes, that means fighting the problem head-on. Other times, it's better to flee the situation. And when we can't do either of those things, our bodies might just shut down, going into a state of "freeze." In the most intense moments, we might even dissociate, which is like our minds taking a mini-vacation to keep us safe.

While all of these responses may seem overwhelming, they're actually pretty smart. Our bodies and minds are doing what they need to do in order to protect us in the moment. And while it can be tough to confront the trauma that's happened to us, it's a critical step in the healing process. By facing the past, we can begin to move forward and find peace in the present.

Confronting past trauma is a process of facing and dealing

with painful memories and experiences from one's past. It can be a difficult and emotional journey, but it's also a crucial step in healing and personal growth. I HIGHLY recommend you do this with a professional. Having a therapist really helped me to:

Understanding the Impact: Confronting past trauma means understanding the impact it has had on your life and how it has shaped your beliefs, behaviours, and relationships. By exploring these experiences, you can gain insight into why you think, feel, and behave the way you do.

Facing Your Emotions: Confronting past trauma often involves facing and processing intense emotions, such as fear, anger, sadness, and shame. This can be challenging, but it's also a powerful way to release these emotions and heal from the past.

Seeking Support: Confronting past trauma can be difficult to do alone, which is why seeking support is crucial. This can come in the form of therapy, support groups, or talking to trusted friends or family members.

Finding Closure: Confronting past trauma can help you find closure and a sense of resolution. It can be liberating to finally face and deal with your past experiences, and it can lead to greater peace and happiness in your life.

The next chapter focuses on my recommendations of healing and what's worked for me. Obviously, I'm not a doctor so please don't take this as medical advice and always a professional. But based on my personal experience this is what works for me.

LET'S TALK ABOUT TRIGGERS:

You know what they say about the biggest trap in spirituality? It's called "spiritual bypassing," . It's when we use spiritual concepts and practices to dodge our emotional baggage and unresolved issues. Newsflash: you can't move forward in your psycho-spiritual journey until you face those wounds head-on.

But oh no, we resist this process like the plague! Why? Because it means sitting in the hot seat of discomfort and staring our demons in the face. And let me tell you, those wounds are usually from our childhood. Yep, every emotional trigger you've got in your present situation? It's probably a blast from the past.

It's when we try to use our spiritual practices and ideas to escape our emotional or psychological wounds, like a cheap getaway to avoid facing our problems. But let me tell you, that's not how you achieve true psycho-spiritual growth, okay?

See, it's like trying to put a band-aid on a broken bone. You can't just ignore your childhood traumas and expect to heal. Trust me, I've tried. Those emotional triggers do you keep experiencing in your present environment? Yeah, most of them come from your past, and you can't just sweep them under the rug and pretend they're not there.

Here are five ways to know you've been triggered and what to do about it:

1. Physical sensations: When you're triggered, you might feel physical sensations like tightness in your chest, a knot in your stomach, or a pounding heart.
2. Strong emotional reactions: If you find yourself suddenly feeling intense anger, fear, sadness, or other powerful emotions, you may have been triggered.
3. Negative self-talk: You might notice that you're engaging in negative self-talk, such as telling yourself you're stupid, worthless, or unlovable.
4. Unhealthy behaviours: When you're triggered, you may find yourself engaging in unhealthy behaviours, like binge eating, drinking, or substance abuse.
5. Defensive or aggressive behaviour: If you're feeling defensive, attacking others, or shutting down, it may be a sign that you've been triggered.

If you notice any of these signs, take a step back and try to identify what triggered you. Once you've identified the trigger, take some time to breathe deeply and calm your nervous system. You can also try journaling or talking to a trusted friend or therapist about what you're feeling. Practising self-care and self-compassion can also be helpful. Remember that being triggered is a normal part of the human experience, and with some self-awareness and support, you can learn to navigate these challenging moments with greater ease.

QUESTIONING YOUR REALITY:

Questioning reality during a spiritual awakening is a common experience for many people. As you start to awaken to a deeper understanding of yourself and the world around you, you may find that your old perceptions of reality no longer hold up.

You may start to question everything you once believed to be true, including the nature of reality itself. This can be a scary and disorienting experience, but it can also be incredibly liberating.

As you begin to question reality, you may start to see things from a new perspective. You may begin to understand that the reality you once believed in is just one of many possible realities, and that there is much more to life than what meets the eye.

So, if you're going through a spiritual awakening and finding yourself questioning reality, embrace it. Allow yourself to explore these new perspectives and ideas. You may be surprised by what you discover!

It can definitely feel lonely when you're the only one questioning reality during a spiritual awakening. It's a unique experience that not everyone will understand or relate to, and that can be isolating.

However, it's important to remember that you're not alone in this. Many people go through similar experiences during their own spiritual awakenings. While the details may be different, the feeling of questioning reality and feeling like an outsider is something that many people can relate to.

So, don't be afraid to reach out and connect with others who may be going through a similar experience. There are plenty of online communities, support groups, and spiritual organizations that can offer a sense of connection and belonging during this time.

And remember, questioning reality is a courageous and important step in your spiritual journey. It's through questioning and exploring that we can find new truths and deeper understanding. So embrace this phase of your journey, even if it feels a little lonely at times.

Your thoughts have a powerful impact on your reality. They shape your beliefs, which in turn influence your actions and the decisions you make. If you constantly think negative thoughts, you'll likely feel stuck and limited in your life. When you experience trauma, your brain and body go into survival mode to help you cope with the situation. This can result in conditioned responses that may not serve you in your everyday life. For example, you may have developed hypervigilance, anxiety, or avoidance behaviours as a result of your trauma.

It's important to acknowledge and address these conditioned responses before you can effectively work on manifesting your goals. Healing from trauma involves addressing and processing the emotions and beliefs that have been stored in your body and mind. This may involve seeking therapy, practicing self-care, and engaging in healing practices such as meditation or yoga.

By addressing the trauma and healing from it, you can begin to recondition your brain and develop new, more positive patterns of thought and behaviour. This will help you to approach life from a more grounded and balanced place, which will ultimately support your ability to manifest your goals in a more sustainable and fulfilling way.

This is because your thoughts create energy that vibrates at a certain frequency. And according to the law of attraction, the universe responds to this energy by bringing similar energy back to you. So if you're constantly thinking about how you don't have enough money, you're actually attracting more lack and scarcity into your life.

In fact, it's normal to have negative thoughts and emotions from time to time. However, it's important to be mindful of the thoughts that you consistently hold onto and the impact they can have on your life.

If you constantly dwell on negative thoughts and beliefs, they can become ingrained in your subconscious mind and affect the way you view yourself and the world around you. This can lead to a self-fulfilling prophecy, where your negative thoughts become your reality.

On the other hand, if you consistently focus on positive thoughts and beliefs, you'll be more likely to take action towards your goals and attract positive outcomes into your life. This doesn't mean that you have to be happy and optimistic all the time, but it does mean that you should be aware of your thoughts and actively work towards cultivating a positive mindset.

CHAPTER 3: HEALING AND FEELING

Life is unpredictable, and no one is immune to its negative experiences. No matter who you are, where you come from, or what you do, life's challenges are bound to come knocking at your door. The loss of a loved one, a breakup, a job loss, an illness, or financial difficulties are just some of the challenges that we may encounter. These experiences can be incredibly tough to go through, but they are a part of life that we all have to deal with.

It is easy to think that some people are luckier than others and that they have it easier. However, this is not always the case. We all have our own struggles, and it's important to remember that we never really know what others are going through. Some people may be better at masking their pain or difficulties, but everyone faces their own set of challenges. Therefore, it is important to be kind and empathetic towards others, as we all need a little support and understanding from time to time.

When it comes to tough experiences, we often hear the terms "small t" and "big T" traumas. Small t traumas are things that may not be life-threatening, but can still really impact us emotionally. These could be things like going through a bad breakup, dealing with bullying, or experiencing emotional abuse. Even though they may not seem as intense as big T traumas, they can still cause a lot of distress and have long-lasting effects on our well-being.

On the other hand, big T traumas are events that are usually life-threatening or cause a lot of emotional distress. These could be things like surviving a natural disaster, experiencing physical abuse or sexual assault, or losing someone you love suddenly. These types of experiences can cause severe emotional and psychological problems, such as PTSD or depression.

It's important to remember that everyone's experience with trauma is unique, and what may be traumatic for one person may not be for another. Additionally, there are a lot of different factors that can affect how trauma impacts us, such as our age, previous exposure to trauma, and the amount of support we have around us.

Even though small t traumas may not seem as severe as big T traumas, it's still important to take them seriously and get support if you need it. Speaking to a mental health professional can be really helpful if you've been through a tough experience, no matter what kind of trauma it was. Remember, you're not alone and there are people who can help you through difficult times.

Whether you've experienced a big T trauma or a small t trauma, it's important to confront that experience and work on healing from it. Trauma can affect us in many ways and can hold us back from reaching our full potential.

By facing and processing the traumatic event, we can start to gain a deeper understanding of how it has impacted us and begin to move forward. This can involve seeking support from a mental health professional, practicing self-care, and working on developing coping strategies that can help us deal with any ongoing emotional challenges.

While it may be difficult and take time, the process of healing from trauma is essential for our well-being and personal growth. It can help us break free from thought patterns and behaviours that may be keeping us stuck in the past and allow us to move forward with a greater sense of clarity, self-awareness, and resilience.

For 30 years, I wasn't really feeling anything. It was so much easier for me to block out my feelings because the more I felt, the more emotions and memories from my past traumas would surface. I tried to suppress them, but it only made suppression easier. Although it wasn't easy to live with, it was what worked for me and got me through it.

Here are some of the ways I avoided feeling:

1. Avoidance - I might avoid situations or people that trigger uncomfortable emotions, or distract myself with other activities to avoid feeling those emotions.
2. Rationalisation - I might try to rationalise or justify my emotions by telling myself that they're not that important or that I shouldn't feel that way.
3. Numbing - I overworked or overspent, to numb or suppress my emotions.

As someone who struggled with low self-worth and found myself in toxic relationships and work environments, I didn't prioritise healing for a long time. I didn't think I was worth the effort and didn't believe that healing would make a difference. This mindset can be common for many people who have experienced trauma or struggle with mental health issues. We may believe that we don't deserve to feel better or that nothing can truly help us. It can take time and effort to change this belief and begin prioritising our own healing and well-being.

But when we take the time to heal, we're taking control of our lives and our well-being. We're saying, "I deserve to feel happy and healthy, damn it!" And that's a powerful thing. Healing is like the foundation of a damn building - without it, everything else is gonna crumble. So, let me spill the tea in my chapter on why healing is so important in my spiritual awakening book.

Healing can help us let go of emotional baggage, release limiting beliefs, and become more resilient in the face of life's challenges. It can help us to develop healthier relationships with ourselves and with others, and to live our lives with greater purpose and meaning.

Avoiding your healing journey because of fear is like avoiding the gym because you're afraid of sweat. Sure, facing your traumas and emotions can be scary, but trust me, NOT facing them is even scarier in the long run.

Suppressed emotions are feelings and emotions that we consciously or unconsciously choose not to express or deal with. When we suppress our emotions, we try to hide, ignore, or avoid them, instead of acknowledging and processing them.

Suppressing our emotions can lead to various negative consequences, both in our physical and mental health. Emotions that are suppressed can build up over time, leading to increased stress, anxiety, and depression. This can lead to physical symptoms like headaches, digestive problems, and chronic pain.

Suppressing our emotions can also impact our relationships with others, as we may have difficulty expressing our needs and communicating effectively. Over time, this can lead to misunderstandings, conflicts, and even isolation.

It's important to acknowledge and express our emotions in a healthy way, as this allows us to process and release them. This can involve talking with a trusted friend or therapist, engaging in creative activities, or simply allowing ourselves to feel and express our emotions in a safe and healthy way.

Those suppressed emotions and wounds can fester and grow like a nasty infection, affecting every aspect of your life. So, embrace the fear, take the leap, and start your healing journey - because the end result is a happier, healthier, and more fulfilled you.

Alright, let's break it down: healing is not a one-size-fits-all situation, no matter what anyone tells you. Sure, there are some techniques and guidelines out there, but ultimately, it's up to you to figure out what works best for you and your unique situation. And let me tell you, healing is anything but straightforward. It's more like a rollercoaster ride with twists and turns and unexpected drops. So if you're looking for a checklist or a step-by-step guide to healing, you might as well toss that out the window. It's a personal journey that requires constant adjustments and new discoveries, so get ready to embrace the individuality of it all. It is essential to approach healing as a journey, rather than a destination with a fixed timeline and cost. It requires patience, self-care, and a commitment to growth and well-being. It is also crucial to seek professional help from trained experts in the field to guide you through the process and ensure a safe and effective healing journey.

If you're ready to face your life head-on and demolish those walls and coping mechanisms you've built up, then healing can be all yours! But let's get real, when tough times or trauma hit, we all react in some way. Fear and anxiety might grip you, leaving you constantly on edge. Your energy levels could skyrocket or plummet, depending on whether you try to control everything or avoid it all. And don't even get me started on avoidance - it's like a one-way ticket to depression town. But don't worry, feeling grief, shame, guilt, and self-abuse aren't freakish reactions - they're just natural parts of the healing process. Because let's be honest, it takes some work to forgive and let go of the past.

But here's the thing - healing demands that we face our circumstances head-on and learn to create a new way forward. The tough times have the power to change us for better or worse, and it's up to us to decide which way we go. So, once you've recognised that it's time to take charge of your healing journey, you can start asking yourself - where do I begin?

The following is what works for me, but I encourage you to experiment and find what healing techniques work best for you. It's important to remember that healing is not a one-size-fits-all process and that what may work for one person may not work for another. So, take the time to explore different methods and find what resonates with you on your journey towards healing and self-discovery.

CHAKRA HEALING:

A key way to make sure you're aligned and healing, is to heal the Chakras.The concept of chakras originated in ancient India, specifically within the Hindu and Buddhist traditions. The word "chakra" comes from Sanskrit and means "wheel" or "disk". The chakras are believed to be energy centers within the body that are located along the spine, with each chakra corresponding to different physical, emotional, and spiritual aspects of a person's being.

The earliest written references to chakras can be found in the Vedas, ancient Indian texts dating back to around 1500 BCE. The chakra system was further developed in the Upanishads and the Yoga Sutras, two influential Hindu texts written between 800 BCE and 400 CE.
Buddhism, which originated in India in the 6th century BCE, also adopted the concept of chakras and integrated it into their own teachings. The Buddhist chakra system is similar to the Hindu system, but with some variations in the number and location of the chakras.
Over time, the concept of chakras has spread beyond India and has been adopted by many other spiritual and healing traditions around the world, including in the West. Today, the chakra system is widely used in various forms of yoga, meditation, and holistic healing practices.

They're like little energy centres in your body, and they're responsible for keeping you balanced and aligned. But just like anything else, they can get out of whack from time to time, leaving you feeling like a hot mess express. That's where chakra healing comes in.

Chakra healing is all about clearing out any blocked or stagnant energy in your chakras and getting everything flowing smoothly again. And let me tell you when your chakras are on point, life is so much better. You'll feel more grounded, energised, and centred.

WHAT ARE THE CHAKRAS?

It is related to tranquility and considered a symbol of hidden potential. It influences balance, stability, security including self-confidence & vitality. Negative emotions in this chakra represent fear and anxiety while positive emotions manifest as courage, will power & well being.

Chakras can become blocked due to a variety of factors, including physical, emotional, and spiritual imbalances. When a chakra is blocked, the flow of energy within the body is disrupted, which can lead to physical or emotional symptoms. Some common causes of chakra blockages include:

1. Physical issues: A blockage can occur due to physical issues, such as injury, illness, or poor diet. For example, the root chakra, which is located at the base of the spine, can become blocked due to physical issues in the lower body.
2. Emotional issues: Emotional imbalances, such as stress, fear, or grief, can also lead to chakra blockages. For example, the heart chakra, which is located in the chest area, can become blocked due to emotional issues related to love, relationships, or self-acceptance.
3. Spiritual issues: Spiritual imbalances, such as a lack of connection to one's higher self or purpose, can also lead to chakra blockages. For example, the crown chakra, which is located at the top of the head, can become blocked due to a lack of spiritual connection or purpose.

4. Environmental factors: Environmental factors, such as pollution or electromagnetic radiation, can also disrupt the flow of energy within the body and lead to chakra blockages.

There are many techniques you can use to clear your chakras, depending on your personal preferences and the specific chakras that need balancing. Here are some common techniques that you can try:

1. Meditation: One of the simplest and most effective ways to balance your chakras is through meditation. You can find many guided meditations online that focus on each of the chakras. Simply find a quiet place, sit comfortably, and focus your attention on the chakra you want to balance.

2. Yoga: Yoga is another great way to balance your chakras, as it combines physical movement with breathwork and meditation. There are many yoga poses that target specific chakras, such as the Tree pose for the root chakra, the Camel pose for the heart chakra, and the Lotus pose for the crown chakra.

3. Energy healing: Energy healing techniques, such as Reiki or acupuncture, can help to balance the chakras by removing blockages and restoring the flow of energy within the body.

4. Affirmations: Affirmations are positive statements that can help to shift your mindset and balance your chakras. For example, you can repeat the affirmation "I am safe and grounded" to balance your root chakra, or "I am open to receiving love and joy" to balance your heart chakra.

5. Essential oils: Certain essential oils, such as lavender for the crown chakra or peppermint for the third eye chakra, can help to balance the chakras when used in aromatherapy or applied topically.

Remember that chakra balancing is a process, and it may take time to fully clear any blockages. You may need to experiment with different techniques and find what works best for you. It's also important to maintain a healthy lifestyle, such as eating a balanced diet, staying hydrated, getting enough sleep, and practicing self-care, to support your overall well-being and keep your chakras balanced.

THE DIFFERENT CHAKRAS:

ROOT CHAKRA

The sacral chakra is located just below your belly button and connects with your emotions, sense of creativity and sense of well-being. It also relates to our sense of self and what we need to do to keep our bodies functioning properly. It has feminine energy to it and governs our passion both sexually and creatively.

SACRAL CHAKRA

The sacral chakra is located just below your belly button and connects with your emotions, sense of creativity and sense of well-being. It also relates to our sense of self and what we need to do to keep our bodies functioning properly. It has feminine energy to it and governs our passion both sexually and creatively.

The Sacral Chakra represents creativity and being open to possibilities and realities in the spirit world. It is said to govern creativity and can help creative abilities flow into all the other chakras, including the throat, heart and third eye chakra.

It balances or neutralises energy or emotions and blocks you from releasing obsessive or negative thoughts, that could lead to regression.

SOLAR PLEXUS CHAKRA

The heart chakra is associated with compassion, affection, and love. The energy of the heart chakra starts in the centre and expands through the chest. This chakra connects the lower and upper chakras, acting as a bridge between earthly matters and higher aspirations

HEART CHAKRA

The heart chakra is located between your heart and your lungs and gives us the ability to feel love and compassion. The fact that it's the centre of the heart is probably why the emotion of love is known as the fifth chakra. It's also the energy that makes you come alive.

The heart chakra is associated with compassion, affection, and love. The energy of the heart chakra starts in the centre and expands through the chest. This chakra connects the lower and upper chakras, acting as a bridge between earthly matters and higher aspirations

The heart chakra as you can imagine is associated with love, from your relationships to your passions, the heart chakra has it all going on. If you experience pain around here, it can be a sign of heartbreak, betrayal or even grief. This is one of the main factors in a blocked chakra and there are many ways to free the energy from this chakra, from Reiki healing to kinesiology and all the energy healing modalities.

Its pattern is typically bluish/ purple, which symbolises composure and peace. Greener hues are seen as the ability to metabolize matter and lower oneself to materialistic pursuits, while white sometimes symbolises clarity or streaming water.

The heart chakra has to do with our relationships and connections with others. If there has been some loss or hurt in relationships, it is felt in the heart area. The loss or hurt could even be associated with things and events, such as moving or losing a job

THROAT CHAKRA

The third eye chakra is primarily related to your inner vision and intuition. People often activate this core when they meditate and frequently use it when they have higher level psychic abilities. It's referred to as your superpower centre.

THIRD EYE CHAKRA

The third eye chakra is primarily related to your inner vision and intuition. People often activate this core when they meditate and frequently use it when they have higher-level psychic abilities. It's referred to as your superpower centre.

CROWN CHAKRA

If you're ready to face your life head-on and demolish those walls and coping mechanisms you've built up, then healing can be all yours! But let's get real, when tough times or trauma hit, we all react in some way. Fear and anxiety might grip you, leaving you constantly on edge. Your energy levels could skyrocket or plummet, depending on whether you try to control everything or avoid it all. And don't even get me started on avoidance - it's like a one-way ticket to depression town. But don't worry, feeling grief, shame, guilt, and self-abuse aren't freakish reactions - they're just natural parts of the healing process. Because let's be honest, it takes some work to forgive and let go of the past.

HOLISTIC THERAPY

Holistic therapy is all about treating the whole person, not just their symptoms. It's a way to connect the mind, body, and spirit to promote overall well-being and healing.

So, what does that actually mean? Well, instead of just looking at physical symptoms or specific mental health diagnoses, holistic therapy takes into account your entire lifestyle, including your habits, beliefs, and environment. It's about looking at the big picture and figuring out what's contributing to your overall health (or lack thereof).

Holistic therapy can involve a variety of different practices, depending on your needs and preferences. Some common examples include acupuncture, meditation, yoga, massage, and nutrition counseling. The idea is to find a combination of approaches that work for you and support your individual healing journey.

I had an amazing therapy experience with someone who was truly in tune with the spiritual, physical, and mental aspects of my well-being. Their approach was way ahead of its time, and they had a profound impact on me by using a lot of empathy and helping me put words to what I was going through.

It's essential to find the right therapist, especially if you've had negative experiences in therapy before. When you've been gaslit and made to feel bad about what happened to you, it can be incredibly challenging to open up to someone new and trust them with your emotional well-being.

Finding the right therapist means finding someone who is a

good fit for you and who you feel comfortable with. This may take some time, but it's important not to give up. A therapist who specialises in trauma and has experience working with individuals who have been through similar experiences can make a world of difference.

A good therapist should never make you feel invalidated, belittled, or judged. Instead, they should create a safe space for you to express your feelings and work through your trauma at your own pace. They should be empathetic and patient, allowing you to build trust and feel comfortable in the therapeutic relationship.

It's also important to remember that finding the right therapist is a process. You may have to try out a few different therapists before you find someone who is the right fit for you. Don't be afraid to ask questions and be upfront about what you're looking for in a therapist. Ultimately, the goal is to find someone who can support you in your healing journey and help you move forward in a positive way.

When you find the right therapist, you just know. Here are five ways that can help you figure out if you've found the right fit:

1. They get you: You know you've found the right therapist when they really "get" you - when they understand your experiences and can relate to what you're going through. You feel like you're not alone in the world and that someone is truly listening to you.
2. They make you feel seen: A good therapist will make you feel seen and heard. You know you've found the right fit when you leave each session feeling like you've been seen for who you really are - flaws and all.
3. They challenge you: A great therapist will challenge you to push yourself and grow in ways that you never thought possible. They'll gently nudge you out of your comfort zone and help you build the skills you need to tackle life's challenges head-on.

4. They don't put up with your BS: Let's be real - sometimes we all need someone to call us out on our BS. You know you've found the right therapist when they're not afraid to challenge your negative thought patterns or behaviours and help you work through them in a positive way.

5. You feel like you can be yourself: Finally, you know you've found the right therapist when you feel like you can be your authentic self in their presence. You don't have to put on a front or pretend to be someone you're not - you can just be yourself and know that you're accepted and supported.

REIKI AND ENERGY HEALING

Reiki is all about using the power of touch and intention to channel healing energy into your body, helping to unblock any energetic gunk that might be holding you back. And when it comes to chakras, Reiki can help to balance and align them, making sure that your energy is flowing smoothly and evenly throughout your body. Plus, it can also help to clear and cleanse your auric field, which is like the energetic bubble that surrounds you, protecting you from negative vibes and outside influences.

This was one of the most powerful ways of getting started in my healing experiment. And I went to see a friend of a friend and she was really really powerful. Because she is quite shamanic by nature, she also spotted other influences in my body that needed attention. Such as the entity that I mentioned that was attached to me. I went to quite a few sessions with Katie, and they were all done virtually. At first I wasn't sure how that was going to work, because I've never done it before, so you kinda doubt it, right? But it was like I was in the room with her. I could actually feel her hands on me, even though she was all the way across the city in a different house.

See, when it comes to energy, time and space are just suggestions. That's right, the Reiki energy doesn't care if you're in the same room as the practitioner or on the other side of the world - it's gonna work its mojo either way.

So, how does this virtual Reiki thing work? Well, it's all about intention and connection, baby. The practitioner sets their intention to send the energy your way, and then they use their skills and experience to tap into that energy and direct it towards you, no matter where you are in the world. It's like the energy is riding a cosmic wave through the universe and landing right where it needs to be.

And let me tell you, just because you're not in the same room as the practitioner doesn't mean you're missing out on anything. You'll still get all the same benefits of the Reiki energy, like deep relaxation, emotional release, and spiritual growth. Plus, you get to do it all from the comfort of your own home - no pants required!

So if you're skeptical about this whole virtual Reiki thing, just remember: energy doesn't play by the rules of time and space. And when it comes to the power of the Reiki, distance is just a number, baby.

Reiki therapy is all about tapping into your body's natural self-healing abilities by guiding energy throughout it. The practitioner is just a conduit for the healing energy - like a garden hose for water, you feel me? It's not about the practitioner causing the healing - they're just there to help you get in touch with your inner power and make it rain, energetically speaking.

Now, when it comes to trauma, Reiki can be an absolute game-changer. It can help to release any pent-up emotions and energetic blockages that might be stuck in your body, allowing you to process and heal from past experiences. And because Reiki is non-invasive and gentle, it can be a great option for folks who might be wary of more traditional forms of therapy.

There are also a set of Reiki symbols that some practitioners use. These symbols are like power-ups for the Reiki energy they help the practitioner tap into different aspects of the healing energy and make it work even better. We're talking more balance, more harmony, more connection, you name it.

Now, during a Reiki session, the practitioner might draw 'em in the air, visualize them in their mind's eye, or chant their names. And all the while, they're channelling that Reiki energy your way and using the symbols to turbocharge the healing process.

It's important to note that not every Reiki practitioner uses these symbols, but for those who do, they can be a game-changer. So if you're ready to level up your healing game, find yourself a practitioner who knows their Cho Ku Rei from their Sei He Ki and get ready to feel the power of those Reiki symbols in action.

Here's a step-by-step breakdown of what typically happens in a Reiki session:

1. First, the practitioner will likely have a conversation with you to discuss your reasons for seeking Reiki and any specific concerns or issues you'd like to address.
2. Next, you'll typically be asked to lie down on a comfortable table or mat, fully clothed.
3. The practitioner will begin by using their hands to lightly touch or hover over different areas of your body, starting from your head and working down to your feet.
4. As they do this, they'll be using specific hand positions and techniques to channel Reiki energy into your body.
5. You may feel sensations such as warmth, tingling, or relaxation as the energy flows through you.
6. The practitioner may also use different tools, such as crystals or essential oils, to enhance the healing energy.
7. Throughout the session, the practitioner will

      continue to adjust their hand positions and techniques based on your energy and any feedback you give them.

8. The session will typically last around 60-90 minutes, depending on the practitioner and your individual needs.

9. After the session, the practitioner may offer you water or some time to rest and integrate the experience.

Overall, Reiki sessions are designed to be relaxing and nurturing, and the specific experience can vary depending on the practitioner and your own unique energy. But regardless of the details, the goal is always the same: to help you tap into your body's innate healing abilities and find a greater sense of balance and well-being.

EFT: EMOTIONAL FREEDOM TECHNIQUE

Emotional Freedom Technique, or EFT for short, is like a triple threat of therapy, using cognitive, exposure, and acupressure techniques to help you deal with your emotions. It's all about tapping specific points on your body while focusing on a specific problem or feeling, because it's believed that emotional turmoil can mess with your body's energy flow.

So, what are the perks of tapping away your problems? Well, EFT can help you chill out and ease anxiety, depression, and chronic pain, and even help you catch some zzz's. Plus, it's super easy to learn and can be done in just a few minutes, making it perfect for anyone who's got a busy schedule but still wants to take care of their mental health.

When I first tried it, I thought, "Am I crazy for tapping on my face and body like a weirdo?" But I soon realised that this technique was actually helping me release built-up energy and emotions in a way that felt pretty damn good. I mean, who doesn't love a good yawn and a few tears to release some stress?

And the best part? You can pair the tapping with affirmations to retrain your subconscious mind and help you develop some new, positive thought patterns. It's like a double whammy of healing goodness. So, next time you're feeling stressed or overwhelmed, don't be afraid to tap it out and affirm your way to a better mental state.

I learned to do it with spiritual pop star and all-around unicorn Gala Darling .

Gala is a New Zealand-born author, speaker, and teacher who is known for her work in the self-help and personal development space. She is the author of the book "Radical Self-Love: A Guide to Loving Yourself and Living Your Dreams," and has also created various online courses and programs on topics such as manifesting, self-love, and creativity.

Gala started her career as a fashion blogger but later transitioned into the personal development space after experiencing her own struggles with depression and anxiety. She began sharing her journey of self-discovery and self-love on her blog, which quickly gained a following.

Gala's approach to self-development and spirituality is different from the traditional and often boring methods. She infuses creativity, humour, and excitement into her teachings, making them more relatable and accessible to a wider audience. Her use of social media and other digital platforms has helped her reach a global audience, inspiring people from all walks of life to live their best lives.

For many people, including myself, Gala's work has been life-changing. Her emphasis on self-love and acceptance, as well as her practical tools such as the Emotional Freedom Technique (EFT), have helped many individuals overcome limiting beliefs, heal past traumas, and achieve personal growth.

Personally, I found Gala's teachings and the use of EFT tapping to be incredibly helpful in my own healing journey. The tapping helped me to reprogram my brain and release negative emotions, which in turn helped to alleviate my suicidal thoughts and feelings of hopelessness. And the fact that her approach to self development was modern and fun, made it much easier for me to connect with and implement in my life.

Now, if you want to give it a go, here's what you need to do: first, figure out what issue or feeling you want to tackle. Then, rate the intensity of that emotion on a scale of 0 to 10. Next, use your fingertips to tap on specific acupressure points while repeating a phrase related to your issue or emotion. The points to tap include the eyebrow, side of the eye, under the eye, under nose, chin, collarbone, under the arm, and top of the head.

After a few rounds of tapping, take a deep breath and rate the intensity of your emotion again. Keep tapping until you feel more chill and your emotions are at a comfortable level. Repeat this process whenever you need to manage your emotions and feel better.

KINESIOLOGY

Kinesiology is a holistic therapy that uses muscle testing to identify imbalances in the body's energy and to help restore balance and health. It's like a detective game for your body - the practitioner uses gentle pressure on your muscles to see how your body responds, and from there they can pinpoint areas of stress or tension.

But it's not just about the muscles - kinesiology takes a whole-body approach to healing. It looks at the physical, emotional, and spiritual aspects of your being, and uses muscle testing to identify underlying issues that may be causing imbalances. Then, the practitioner can use a variety of techniques to help restore balance and promote healing, like acupressure, nutritional advice, and emotional release.

Basically, kinesiology is all about empowering you to take control of your own health and well-being. By tapping into the body's innate wisdom and using muscle testing as a guide, you can identify and release the things that are holding you back and move towards a more balanced, healthy, and joyful life.

During a kinesiology session, you're gonna be the star of the show, baby. The practitioner will start by asking you some questions about your health and well-being, and getting to know you a little better. Then, they'll get you comfortable on the table and start doing some muscle testing.

Now, don't worry - this ain't no gym class. The muscle testing is gentle and non-invasive. The practitioner will ask you to hold your arm or leg in a certain position while they apply light pressure. They're not trying to make you lift weights or anything like that - they're just checking to see how your muscles respond to different stimuli.

Based on the results of the muscle testing, the practitioner will start to identify areas of stress or imbalance in your body. This might be related to physical issues like pain or tension, or it might be related to emotional or spiritual blocks that are holding you back. From there, they'll use a variety of techniques to help restore balance and promote healing.

These techniques might include acupressure, where the practitioner uses gentle pressure on specific points of your body to release tension and promote relaxation. They might also give you some nutritional advice, or suggest some exercises or stretches to help support your healing. And if there are emotional or spiritual blocks that need to be released, they might use techniques like visualization or guided meditation to help you tap into your own inner wisdom and find the answers you need. They might also incorporate affirmations or positive statements to help shift your mindset and promote healing on a spiritual level. Additionally, the practitioner may use techniques such as chakra balancing, energy work, or other spiritual modalities to help you clear energetic blocks and promote spiritual healing.

See, for years I had been holding onto trauma energy in my body, and it was starting to manifest in some weird ways. I had developed arthritis out of nowhere, and my gut was all kinds of messed up. I didn't even realise that those things could be related to trauma - I just thought my body was randomly falling apart.

But then I went to my kinesiology session, and my practitioner was able to pinpoint the exact areas where that trauma energy was stored in my body. We did some muscle testing and energy work, and let me tell you - I could feel that energy starting to shift and release.

Not only did she do muscle testing and energy work to release my trauma, but she also brought in some acupressure and Reiki energy healing to really take things to the next level.

And let me tell you about the light language - that was some next-level stuff. It's like a spiritual code that bypasses your logical mind and goes straight to your soul. My kinesiologist was speaking in tongues, and I swear I could feel the energy shifting and moving around me.

Now, I know some folks might be like "what the heck is light language?" But trust me - it's powerful stuff. When you're dealing with trauma that's been stored in your body for years, sometimes you need something that goes beyond words and logic. And that's where light language comes in.

So if you're dealing with some deep-rooted trauma that you just can't seem to shake, consider trying kinesiology with a practitioner who knows their stuff. Acupressure, Reiki, and light language might just be the missing pieces of the puzzle that you need to finally release that trauma and step into your power.

During my kinesiology session, I was just minding my own business, doing some muscle testing and getting my chakras balanced. But then, outta nowhere, I started having visions of past lives! I'm talking about full-on flashbacks to other lifetimes, with different people, different places, and different experiences.

It wasn't just some random trip down memory lane - it was all connected to the things I needed to heal in this lifetime.

See, when you're in a kinesiology session, your body and your spirit are working together to uncover the root causes of your physical and emotional issues. And sometimes, those root causes go wayyyy back - like, way before this lifetime. That's where the past lives come in.

During my session, my kinesiology practitioner helped me to connect the dots between my past lives and my current issues. We talked about how the things I experienced in those past lives were still affecting me in this lifetime, and how I could use that information to heal and move forward.

Throughout the session, the practitioner will be working with you as a team . They'll be listening to your body's responses, asking you for feedback, and making adjustments as needed. And by the end of the session, you'll be feeling more balanced, more relaxed, and more in tune with your own body's wisdom.

PLANT MEDICINE:

Mother Earth has got our back when it comes to healing. She's got an abundance of goodies that we need to get ourselves feeling right - and a lot of it comes straight from nature. I'm talking about herbs, roots, fruits, flowers, and so much more. These bad boys are packed with all the nutrients, vitamins, and minerals we need to boost our immune system, soothe our minds, and heal our bodies. And let's not forget about nature's other gifts - fresh air, sunlight, and natural water sources.

Plant medicine is the real deal - it's using the healing power of plants to treat everything from physical ailments to mental health issues. We're talking herbs, roots, flowers, and other botanical goodies that have been used for centuries to help people feel their best. And let me tell you, these plants are packing some serious power - they can help with everything from boosting your immune system to reducing stress and anxiety. A lot of folks out there think that plant medicine is just Ayahuasca - like that's the only way to tap into the healing power of plants. But let me tell you, that couldn't be further from the truth.

I have never tried an Ayahuasca ceremony. We're talking about a powerful psychedelic brew made from plants that grow in the Amazon rainforest. Ayahuasca has been used for centuries in traditional healing ceremonies by indigenous people in South America. The brew contains a potent psychoactive compound that can induce intense visions and emotional experiences, and it's said to have the power to heal both physical and emotional ailments. I have however known a lot of people that have gone and done the ceremonies and it's completely changed their life, helped them heal addictions, and get over traumas they never thought they would. And they say that doing a session is like 10 years of therapy in one night. It can be very very intense.

Now, let me be clear - this isn't something to mess around with. Ayahuasca is a powerful medicine, and it should only be taken under the guidance of a trained shaman or experienced practitioner in a safe and supportive environment. It's not a quick fix or a party drug - it's a serious healing practice that requires respect and intention. So, if you're thinking about exploring the world of ayahuasca, make sure you do your research and find a reputable practitioner who can guide you on your journey.

I have tried using functional mushrooms they're the amazing for your health and well-being. These magical little fungi are packed with nutrients and antioxidants that can help boost your immune system, reduce inflammation, and even improve your brain function.

First up, we've got lion's mane. Not only does it sound majestic as hell, but it also boosts cognitive function and has been found to improve memory and focus. So, if you're tired of feeling scatterbrained and forgetful, lion's mane is your new BFF.

Next, we've got the queen of the shrooms - Reishi. This beauty has been shown to reduce stress and anxiety by regulating your body's cortisol levels. So, if you're feeling overwhelmed and need to calm the f*ck down, Reishi has got your back.

And let's not forget about Chaga. This bad boy is a powerhouse of antioxidants, helping to boost your immune system and protect against cell damage. But it also has mood-boosting properties, helping to reduce feelings of depression and anxiety.

But that's not all. These functional mushrooms have also been shown to have benefits for your mental health. They can help reduce stress, anxiety, and depression, and even improve your mood and overall sense of well-being. Who knew a little shroom could do all that?

And the best part? They're easy to incorporate into your daily routine. Add some mushroom powder to your morning smoothie or brew up a cup of mushroom tea

I've also looked into psychedelic-formed mushrooms in microdosing research and the effects on mental health are amazing. Studies have demonstrated that psilocybin therapy can alleviate symptoms of treatment-resistant depression, obsessive-compulsive disorder, and other mental health conditions. Psilocybin has also demonstrated efficacy in reducing fear and anxiety in individuals with terminal cancer. However, because Schedule I substances are challenging to study, many of these investigations have been conducted by Johns Hopkins Medicine. They established the world's most extensive psychedelic research centre, The Center for Psychedelic and Consciousness Research, in 2019, the first psychedelic research centre in the United States.

According to a Johns Hopkins Medicine study, taking psilocybin with talk therapy significantly improved symptoms of clinical depression. Even after receiving only two doses of the substance, some research participants continued to experience benefits for up to a year.

When taken in a supportive environment, psilocybin can lead to self-described "spiritual" experiences that generally result in positive changes in a person's attitude, mood, and behaviour. Specifically, psilocybin seems to enhance a personality trait called "openness," which includes sensitivity, imagination, and an appreciation for the values and perspectives of others.

The increased openness observed in people who take psilocybin may be linked to the compound's ability to enhance neuroplasticity, which is the brain's ability to form new connections. Several studies have supported the idea that psilocybin and other psychedelics can induce or enhance neuroplasticity.

Many people have shared personal stories that suggest that this practice can have major benefits for those with mental health issues, as well as promoting overall wellness.

INNER CHILD HEALING

Inner child healing is a therapeutic process that aims to heal the emotional wounds and traumas that we experienced in childhood. It's based on the idea that our childhood experiences shape our beliefs and behaviours as adults, and that healing those experiences can lead to greater emotional well-being and a more fulfilling life.

The process of inner child healing involves reconnecting with the wounded parts of ourselves and providing them with the love, support, and nurturing that they needed but may not have received as children. This can involve things like visualizations, journaling, meditation, and talk therapy.

One technique that is commonly used in inner child healing is called "re-parenting." This involves imagining yourself as the loving and supportive parent that you needed as a child and providing yourself with the comfort, validation, and encouragement that you may not have received from your actual parents.

Another technique that is often used is called "inner child dialogue," where you have a conversation with your inner child to better understand their needs and feelings, and provide them with the validation and support that they need.

The goal of inner child healing is to help you develop a healthier relationship with yourself and with others and to release the emotional baggage and limiting beliefs that may be holding you back in life. It can help you to heal from things like childhood trauma, low self-esteem, anxiety, depression, and other emotional struggles.

If you're interested in exploring inner child healing, it's important to work with a trained therapist or counsellor who can guide you through the process and provide you with the support and tools that you need. They can help you to identify your specific wounds and traumas, and develop a plan for healing and growth that is tailored to your unique needs and circumstances.

There are many exercises that can help with inner child healing, and the best one for you may depend on your specific needs and preferences. However, here is one exercise that you can try:

1. Find a quiet and comfortable space where you won't be disturbed. Sit in a comfortable position and take a few deep breaths to help yourself relax.
2. Close your eyes and imagine that you are standing in front of a door. This door represents the entrance to your inner child's room.
3. When you are ready, open the door and step inside. Take a moment to look around and observe the room. What does it look like? How does it feel?
4. Look for your inner child in the room. They may be hiding or playing. When you see them, approach them with love and compassion.
5. Ask your inner child what they need from you in order to feel safe and loved. Listen to their response without judgment.
6. Once you have listened to your inner child's needs, offer them comfort and reassurance. You can say things like, "I love you," "You are safe," and "I am here for you."
7. Spend some time in the room with your inner child. You can play together, talk, or just be present with them.

8. When you are ready to leave, say goodbye to your inner child and thank them for spending time with you.
9. Close the door and take a few deep breaths to ground yourself. When you are ready, slowly open your eyes.

This exercise can help you connect with and nurture your inner child, and over time, it can help you heal the emotional wounds that may be blocking your personal growth and well-being.

LETTING GO RITUALS

Letting go ceremonies can happen with the full moon and new moon. These ceremonies offer a powerful way to release what no longer serves us and make space for new beginnings. The full moon is all about letting go of what's weighing us down, while the new moon is about setting intentions for what we want to manifest in our lives.

When it comes to letting go ceremonies, you can either do them solo or with a group of your besties. Doing it solo means you get to fully focus on your own intentions and let go of what no longer serves you. Just make sure you set the mood with a peaceful and quiet space, and follow the steps outlined in the previous response.

But, if you're feeling the need for some community support and want to share your intentions with like-minded peeps, then a group ceremony might be the way to go. Not only will you feel all connected and warm inside, but you'll also have the benefit of people cheering you on as you release what's holding you back.

Now, if you're looking to find a group to do a letting-go ceremony with, there are plenty of options out there. You can hit up Google and search for local spiritual or mindfulness groups, or ask your mates if they know of any groups that are into this sort of thing. And, if you're not keen on leaving the comfort of your own home, there are loads of online communities that offer virtual ceremonies.

Just remember, that letting go is a process and it's totally cool to take things at your own pace. So, set your intentions, trust the process, and let the good vibes flow.

Here are some steps to help you create your own letting go ceremony:

1. Set the mood: Find a quiet and comfortable space where you can focus without distractions. Light some candles, burn some incense or sage, and play some calming music to create a peaceful atmosphere.
2. Write it out: Take some time to reflect on what you want to release. Write down your thoughts, feelings, and anything else that comes up for you. Get it all out on paper and don't hold back.
3. Create a ritual: Decide on a ritual that feels meaningful to you. This can be anything from burning your written thoughts to burying them in the earth. The important thing is to do something physical that symbolises letting go.
4. Call in support: If you're comfortable, invite trusted friends or loved ones to join you in the ceremony. You can share your intentions and support each other as you release what no longer serves you.
5. Set your intentions: After you've let go, take some time to set your intentions for what you want to manifest in your life. Write them down and keep them somewhere you can see them daily.

You can also try cord cutting as part of letting go. The concept of cord cutting is based on the belief that we are all connected energetically and that our thoughts, emotions, and actions can create cords or attachments between ourselves and other people, places, or things. These energetic cords can be positive or negative, and they can impact our physical, emotional, and spiritual well-being.

Positive cords can be formed between individuals who share a strong bond or connection, such as between a parent and child, or between close friends or romantic partners. These cords can create feelings of love, support, and emotional closeness, and can help to strengthen relationships.

However, negative cords can also be formed between individuals who have a toxic or unhealthy relationship, such as between an abusive partner or a controlling parent. These cords can create feelings of fear, anger, and emotional pain, and can have a detrimental impact on our mental and emotional health.

Cord cutting exercises are designed to help individuals release negative attachments or connections that may be holding them back from living a fulfilling and happy life. By visualising the energetic cord and cutting it, individuals can release the negative energy and emotions associated with that attachment, and free themselves from its hold.

They can be particularly helpful for individuals who have experienced trauma or abuse, as these experiences can create strong and negative cords that may be difficult to release. Additionally, cord cutting exercises can be used for releasing negative attachments to places or things, such as a job, a home, or a past experience.

If you're interested in cord cutting and would like to try out some exercises, there are various techniques you can explore. Below are a few examples to get you started.

1. Imagining the cord in ropes:
a. Find a quiet and comfortable space where you won't be disturbed. Sit in a comfortable position and take a few deep breaths to help yourself relax.
b. Close your eyes and visualize the person or situation that you wish to release from your life. Imagine that there is a cord connecting you to this person or situation.
c. Visualize the cord as a rope, with knots or ties binding you to the person or situation.

d. When you are ready, imagine yourself untying the knots or unbinding the rope. As you do this, say a simple statement such as "I release you" or "I am free from this attachment."

e. Visualize the cord falling away from your body and disappearing. Take a few deep breaths and feel the sensation of release and freedom.

2. Burning the connections between you:

a. Find a quiet and comfortable space where you won't be disturbed. Sit in a comfortable position and take a few deep breaths to help yourself relax.

b. Close your eyes and visualize the person or situation that you wish to release from your life. Imagine that there is a cord connecting you to this person or situation.

c. Visualize the cord as a chain, with links connecting you to the person or situation.

d. When you are ready, imagine yourself holding a torch or a lighter. Light the flame and visualize the heat burning through the links of the chain, until it falls apart.

e. As the chain falls apart, say a simple statement such as "I release you" or "I am free from this attachment."

f. Visualize the cord falling away from your body and disappearing. Take a few deep breaths and feel the sensation of release and freedom.

3. Cord cutting with candles:

a. Find a quiet and comfortable space where you won't be disturbed. Sit in a comfortable position and take a few deep breaths to help yourself relax.

b. Light one or more candles in front of you. Choose a color that represents the emotion or situation that you wish to release.

c. Close your eyes and visualize the person or situation that you wish to release from your life. Imagine that there is a cord connecting you to this person or situation.

d. Visualize the cord as a thread of light, extending from your body to the person or situation.

e. When you are ready, imagine yourself holding a pair of scissors or a knife. Cut the cord, and as you do this, visualize the light of the cord being absorbed by the flame of the candle.

f. Repeat the process for each cord that you wish to cut. As you cut each cord, say a simple statement such as "I release you" or "I am free from this attachment."

g. Once you have cut all the cords, take a few deep breaths and feel the sensation of release and freedom.

Remember that cord cutting exercises are meant to be empowering and healing, and it is important to approach them with a mindset of love, compassion, and forgiveness, rather than anger or resentment towards the person or situation.

Letting go is a process, and it's not always easy. Be kind to yourself and take things at your own pace. With practice, you'll find that letting go becomes easier, and you'll be able to create more space for the things you truly want in your life.

Let's set the record straight about letting go. Just because you're ready to move on doesn't mean you have to forgive anyone - especially if they don't deserve it. Don't let anyone preach to you about forgiveness without knowing the whole story - that's just some gaslighting BS! You know what's best for you and your healing process, and you don't owe anyone forgiveness if you don't feel it in your heart. So, let go on your own terms, and don't let anyone tell you otherwise.

ACUPUNCTURE:

Acupuncture has been around for thousands of years, originating in ancient China. Acupuncture is a traditional Chinese medical practice that uses thin needles to balance the flow of energy or "qi" throughout the body. It's been around for over 2,500 years and is a key part of traditional Chinese medicine, which also includes things like herbal medicine and massage.

According to legend, acupuncture was discovered by a Chinese doctor named Bian Que, who found certain points on the body could help alleviate pain and treat illness. The practice gradually spread throughout Asia and eventually to Europe and the United States.

Today, many people around the world use acupuncture to help with a variety of health issues. It's been recognized as a safe and effective form of complementary and alternative medicine by the World Health Organisation.

So, what is it exactly?

Acupuncture involves the insertion of thin needles into specific points on the body. The idea is that these points correspond to different organs or systems in the body, and by stimulating them, the body's natural healing mechanisms can kick in. The needles are left in place for anywhere from a few minutes to over an hour, depending on the practitioner and the condition being treated.

Now, I know what you're thinking - "Doesn't that hurt?" But trust me, , it's not as bad as it sounds. Most people report feeling a mild sensation or pressure when the needles are inserted, but it's not typically painful. Plus, the benefits are well worth it.

So, what are the benefits of acupuncture? Well, there's a laundry list of potential benefits, including pain relief, stress reduction, improved sleep, and increased energy levels. Some people even swear by acupuncture for treating anxiety, depression, and other mental health conditions.

But how does it work, you ask? The theory behind acupuncture is that the needles stimulate the body's flow of "qi" (pronounced "chee"), or life force energy. When this energy flow is blocked or disrupted, it can lead to pain or illness. By restoring the flow of qi, acupuncture can help the body heal itself and restore balance. And while it's often used to treat physical ailments, it can also be a game-changer for emotional and psychological healing.

Trauma can show up in all kinds of ways, from chronic pain to anxiety and depression. But acupuncture can work wonders by regulating your nervous system and balancing out your energy flow. By getting things back in sync, acupuncture can help alleviate those gnarly symptoms and give you the space you need to heal.

If you're dealing with post-traumatic stress disorder (PTSD), acupuncture might be your new BFF. One study found that it can reduce symptoms like hyperarousal and intrusive thoughts. And if you're already working with a therapist or other healing modalities, acupuncture can be a bomb addition to your toolkit. It can help release tension and stress from your body, making it easier to work through those tough emotions.

I've only been to acupuncture a few times, but I've absolutely loved the experience. It's amazing how much it can help release pent-up negative energy or trauma that may have accumulated in my body, whether from this life or past lives. I've found that acupuncture is a great way to get the energy force flowing and promote healing.

During an acupuncture session, the practitioner inserts thin needles into specific points on my body. At first, I was a little nervous about the needles, but the process is actually quite gentle and painless. Once the needles are in place, I usually lay there for around 30 minutes while they work their magic.

After the session, I always feel a noticeable physical and mental effect. I feel more relaxed and centered, like a weight has been lifted off my shoulders. I've noticed that I sleep better and have more energy in the days following acupuncture. It's like my body is functioning more efficiently and everything just feels better.

JOURNALING:

Looks like we got ourselves a journaling skeptic turned believer! I didn't always love journaling tbh. And It's no surprise that having your private thoughts read without your consent as a child and young adult didn't exactly give me warm and fuzzy feelings about writing things down on paper. But, as they say, time heals all wounds and I've found my way back to the journaling game.

Whether you prefer to type or speak your truth, the act of getting those thoughts out of your head and onto a page is incredibly cathartic. Plus, the added bonus of being able to go back and read your past entries and see how much you've grown and changed is pretty damn satisfying.

Some of the benefits of journaling are:

1. First and foremost, journaling is like a cheap therapy session! You get to spill all your juicy thoughts and feelings onto the page without having to fork over hundreds of dollars to a therapist.
2. Journaling helps you get to know yourself on a deeper level . You can start to see patterns in your thoughts and behaviours that you might not have noticed before. It's like having a front-row seat to the inner workings of your mind.
3. Let's face it, life can be overwhelming at times, but journaling gives you a way to process all that chaos. By getting your thoughts out of your head and onto the page, you can start to make sense of the madness and feel more in control of your life.

4. Have you ever had a problem that you just couldn't solve no matter how hard you tried? Well, grab your journal, because the act of writing things down can help you come up with creative solutions and fresh perspectives that you might not have considered before.

5. Last but not least, journaling is just plain old fun! You get to play with words, doodle and be as creative as you want to be. It's like having your very own personal art project that also happens to be good for your mental health. What's not to love about that?

Sometimes I don't exactly know where to start with journaling, but I'll share some of my Waze and ask myself questions as promised to get deeper on things:

10 questions in dealing with and healing trauma:

1. What traumatic experiences have I been through in my life?
2. How have these experiences affected me emotionally, physically, and mentally?
3. What coping mechanisms have I adopted to deal with my trauma? Have they been helpful or harmful?
4. Have I sought professional help to deal with my trauma? If not, what is stopping me from seeking help?
5. What triggers me and reminds me of my trauma? How can I avoid or minimize exposure to these triggers?
6. What self-care practices can I incorporate into my daily routine to help me cope with my trauma?
7. What positive changes have I noticed in myself since I started addressing my trauma?
8. How can I forgive myself and others for the pain caused by my trauma?
9. What actions can I take to move forward and heal

from my trauma?

10. How can I use my experience with trauma to help others who are going through similar experiences?

Journaling questions on spiritual awakening and journey:

1. What does spirituality mean to me?
2. Have I experienced any moments of spiritual awakening in my life?
3. What practices or rituals help me connect to my spirituality?
4. What beliefs or teachings have I adopted on my spiritual journey?
5. What challenges have I faced on my spiritual journey and how have I overcome them?
6. How has my spirituality impacted my relationships, career, or other areas of my life?
7. What do I hope to achieve or experience on my spiritual journey?
8. How can I deepen my connection to my spirituality?
9. What messages or signs have I received from the universe or higher power?
10. How can I integrate my spirituality into my daily life?

Journaling questions on relationships:

1. What patterns do I see in my past relationships?
2. What qualities do I look for in a partner?
3. What are my deal-breakers in a relationship?
4. How do I communicate with my partner when I am upset or hurt?
5. What are my biggest fears or insecurities in relationships?
6. How do I prioritize my own needs while also meeting the needs of my partner?
7. How do I handle conflict in my relationships?
8. What can I do to improve my relationship with my partner?

9. What have I learned from my past relationships that I can bring into my current relationship?
10. What are my goals for my relationship and how can I work towards achieving them?

Journaling questions for limiting beliefs:

1. What is the limiting belief that is holding me back?
2. Where did this belief come from? Who or what influenced me to adopt this belief?
3. What evidence do I have to support this belief? Is this evidence reliable and accurate?
4. What alternative beliefs can I adopt that are more empowering and positive?
5. What actions can I take to reinforce these new beliefs and overcome my limiting beliefs?

So, keep at it, love! Journaling is a safe and sacred space for you to express yourself freely and without judgment. And who knows, maybe one day you'll even feel comfortable enough to bust out a good old-fashioned pen and paper.

CHAPTER 4: SPIRITS, GUIDES AND ANGELS

So if you're ready to take your spiritual journey to the next level, get ready for the ride of your life. We're gonna explore everything from connecting with your spirit guides to channelling your inner badass. And trust me, you're gonna come out the other side a whole new person. So let's do this, boo - grab your crystals and let's get started.

Now, some belief systems think it's a whole separate realm that's crawling with all kinds of non-physical entities - ghosts, spirits, and other spooky beings. But let's be real - that's not everyone's cup of tea.

Personally, I used to be skeptical and scared af about spirits, after a traumatic experience as a kid. But now that I've got my protection game on lock, I'm ready to embrace it all. And let me tell you, there's a lot of good stuff out there to explore.

Here's the deal, though - when you start dabbling in the spirit world, you gotta be careful. Any type of energy can be attracted to yours, and you don't wanna mess with anything that's gonna mess with you. But as long as you're responsible and protect yourself, you'll be good to go.

Before, I never realized the power of protection when it comes to spirituality and connecting with spirits. I remember telling a psychic that I didn't want anything to do with spirits, and I wanted to avoid any kind of involvement with them. That's when she introduced me to the concept of spiritual protection, which I now utilize to my own benefit.

Spiritual protection refers to practices that can help safeguard us against negative energies, entities, or unwanted spiritual experiences. These practices can vary depending on one's beliefs, but they often involve setting intentions, using visualization or meditation techniques, and calling on guides or deities for support.

Since discovering the power of spiritual protection, I've incorporated various protection practices into my spiritual routine. For instance, I always set an intention before meditating or connecting with spirits, asking for protection and guidance. I also visualize myself surrounded by a protective shield of light or imagine myself being surrounded by guardian angels or spirit guides.

By doing so, I feel more confident and secure in my spiritual practice, knowing that I am protected from any negative energies or entities. Additionally, spiritual protection has helped me to become more discerning about the energies I allow into my space, and I feel more in control of my spiritual experiences. I don't mess around when it comes to protecting myself from negative energies or unwanted spirits. I mean, who has time for that kind of drama, right? That's why I've got my secret weapon: the "Activate Shield" technique.

Basically, what I do is say "Activate Shield" and imagine a fabulous pink bubble enveloping me from head to toe. This bubble is like my own personal force field, and it protects me from any and all negative energies or entities that try to mess with my vibe.

I mean, seriously, this pink bubble is the real deal. It's like a big, fluffy pink cloud of protection that follows me wherever I go. And let me tell you, it's saved my ass more times than I can count. Whether I'm dealing with toxic people, bad vibes, or even pesky spirits, this shield has got me covered.

Overall, I believe that spiritual protection is a powerful tool that can help us to navigate the spiritual realm safely and confidently. By incorporating protection practices into our spiritual routine, we can cultivate a sense of safety and empowerment in our spiritual journeys.

So whether you're into ghosts, angels, or anything in between, there's a whole world of spiritual exploration waiting for you. Just keep your wits about you, boo, and get ready for one wild ride.

Some common types of spirits that are believed to exist in the spirit world include:

Ghosts: the spirit or soul of a deceased person that is believed to remain on Earth.

- Ancestors spirits: the spirit of deceased loved ones that are believed to watch over and guide their descendants.
- Nature spirits: spirits that are believed to inhabit natural elements such as rivers, trees, and mountains.
- Guardian spirits: spirits that are believed to protect and guide individuals throughout their lives.
- Demons: malevolent spirits that are believed to cause harm or mischief.
- Angels: benevolent spirits that are believed to act as messengers of God and protectors of humanity.

It's worth noting that belief in the spirit world and types of spirits can vary widely across cultures and religions. Additionally, the concept of the spirit world and the entities within it is often tied to specific religious or spiritual practices, such as ancestor veneration, shamanism, and animism.

Don't let Hollywood fool ya, spirits ain't no joke. But let me tell ya, they can be some serious power players in our lives if we treat them right. Now, I know you've all seen those cheap horror flicks where some kid messes around with an Ouji board and unleashes some "evil" spirit, but let me tell you, spirits ain't evil, they're just misunderstood.

When it comes to communing with spirits, ya gotta have your

wits about ya and know how to protect yourself. And when we talk about spirits, we're talkin' 'bout deceased loved ones, ghosts, and all kinds of entities that exist on the "other side." So, when engaging with these beings, remember to show them the respect you'd want when you're on the other side, not as some spooky ghost, but as a wise, powerful spirit that can guide us. Now, pay attention and take notes, cuz I'm 'bout to tell you the best ways to prepare before contactin' spirits.

Don't even get me started on all the spooky ghost stories floating around out there. But let me tell ya, when we focus on that fearful image, we're just opening ourselves up to all those lower-frequency entities. Trust me, the spirit world is filled with all kinds of trickster spirits that can cause chaos and confusion if we're not careful. You probably don't want to be opening yourself up to just any entity.

Focus on the spirits you actually want to communicate and connect with, and do so with respect and caution. Ya gotta have a clear and calm mindset before engaging in any spiritual work. Anyone can create a connection with their spirits and ancestors, but don't do anything that makes you uncomfortable. Focus on your direct ancestral lineage, as well as spirits you would consider protective guides. Visualize those angels and ancestors that guide you daily, only allowing in those that are in alignment with your highest good.

Before you go gallivanting around any graveyards or cemeteries, let me give you a heads up. Be careful, cuz those restless spirits can attach themselves to you or try to suck the life force right out of ya. You know, the ones that are lost or have unresolved trauma from their lifetime, those are usually the ones we hear about "haunting" people and places. Say a quick prayer for protection for yourself and to leave behind any unwanted entities. That way, no strangers follow you home.

When it comes to interacting with spirits, you gotta be

prepared and know how to protect yourself. Here's a few tips to keep you safe:

1. Set your intentions. Before you start any kind of spiritual work, make sure you set clear intentions and boundaries. Tell any negative or unwanted spirits to stay away. You gotta make it clear to any negative or unwanted spirits that they ain't welcome here. Be specific and assertive, don't be afraid to tell them to stay away and don't hesitate to set your boundaries, this is your spiritual space and you're in charge. Make sure you're clear about what you want, and don't let any negative energy rain on your parade. Trust me, setting your intentions is step one to protecting yourself and getting the most out of your spiritual practice.

Something you can say for protection:

"I call upon my angels, guides and ancestors to protect me from any energy less than fifth-dimensional energy. I am protected, I am strong, and I only allow positive energy to come along."

This mantra is a simple and powerful way to remind yourself of your strength, your protection and positive energy that surrounds you. Repeat it to yourself when you feel a negative energy or unwanted spirit around you, this will help you to focus on the positive and keep the bad spirits away.

1. Shield yourself. Visualise yourself surrounded by a protective white light, or imagine yourself in a bubble of protection. This will create a barrier between you and any unwanted spirits. Think of it like a superhero force field, it's powerful and can repel any negative energy that tries to penetrate it. You can also use this visualisation technique before starting any kind of spiritual work, or when you sense negative energy around you. It's simple, effective and can give you a

sense of control and peace of mind. Trust me, it's like a secret weapon in your spiritual toolbox.

2. Be assertive. If you sense the presence of a negative or unwanted spirit, don't be afraid to tell them to leave. Speak in a strong and confident tone, and make it clear that you don't want them around.

3. Use protective crystals. Certain crystals like black tourmaline, selenite, and amethyst are said to have protective properties. Carry them with you or place them around your home to keep negative energies at bay.

4. Trust your gut. If something doesn't feel right or you sense an eerie presence, listen to that inner voice and get out of there. Trust your intuition, it's there to protect you.

When it comes to dealing with spirits, you're the boss. That's right - you're in charge of your own energy and nobody can mess with that.

If you're feeling like you've got some bad juju hanging around, don't stress. Just find a trusted healer who can help you clear and protect your energy. No need to worry about some crazy exorcism - it's a guided process that will help you feel lighter and more at peace.

Now, let's talk about why entities might be sticking to you like a bad rash. It's all about your energy and aura, baby. When you're feeling down in the dumps with negative emotions like fear, anger, or sadness, you emit a low frequency that these sneaky spirits love to feed on.

But don't worry, you don't have to be a beacon for bad energy forever. Stay assertive, trust your gut, and protect yourself. With a little know-how, you can keep those pesky entities in check and get back to feeling like the boss that you are.

Another reason why entities may attach themselves to certain people is that they are seeking refuge or protection. This is often the case with entities who are lost or afraid and looking for a host to help them feel safe.

In addition, people who engage in activities such as using drugs or alcohol, practicing black magic or other forms of dark magic, and having negative thoughts and intentions can also attract entities. It's important to note that entities do not discriminate and can attach themselves to anyone, regardless of their background or beliefs.

To protect yourself from those pesky entities, you gotta work on keeping your vibes high and your outlook positive. This means getting into some meditation, mindfulness, and surrounding yourself with good juju.

Now, I know what you're thinking - life ain't always sunshine and rainbows, and that's a fact. But I ain't here to tell you to pretend your problems don't exist. What I am saying is that if you've had a rough go of it like me, those bad energy entities are gonna be lining up to get a piece of that low-vibe pie.

That's why it's so important to work on your own healing. Not only will it help you feel better, but it'll keep those pesky spirits at bay. Trust me, you don't wanna deal with the same kind of entity fuckery that I did

There are a number of signs that you may have an entity attached to you, including:

1. Unexplained feelings of anxiety, fear, or negativity: If you suddenly start feeling anxious, afraid, or negative without any logical explanation, it may be a sign of an entity attachment.
2. Sudden changes in behaviour or mood: If you find yourself acting in ways that are out of character, or experiencing sudden changes in mood, this could be a sign of an entity attachment.
3. Physical symptoms: Some people report

experiencing physical symptoms such as headaches, fatigue, or other unexplained health problems when an entity is attached to them.

4. Unusual occurrences in your environment: Some people report strange noises, objects moving on their own, or other unusual occurrences when an entity is attached to them.

5. Unexplained changes in your energy level: If you notice a sudden decrease in energy or an overall feeling of exhaustion, this could be a sign of an entity attachment.

It's important to remember that not everyone who experiences these symptoms has an entity attached to them. Additionally, seeking help from a trusted healer or spiritual practitioner can also help clear any negative energy and entities that may be attached to you.

If you ever find yourself dealing with these types of energies, it's important to know that you don't have to face them alone. Working with a spiritual practitioner or a shaman can help you clear them out and manage them effectively.

If you're not sure where to start, my app Woo Woo can connect you with professionals who are experienced in this type of work. It's always best to work with someone who has training and experience in these matters, as they can guide you through the process safely and effectively.

Remember, your mental and spiritual well-being is important, and there's no shame in seeking help when you need it. Don't hesitate to reach out and get the support you need to clear out those negative energies and keep your energy field healthy and balanced.

YOUR SPIRIT GUIDES

Every single one of us has a squad of spiritual entities helping us navigate this crazy thing we call life. And let me tell you, they can make miracles happen, bringing the perfect people and opportunities right to your doorstep. Your spiritual guidance squad is always sending you advice or clues, like those synchronicities, gut instincts and aha ideas, and the more you listen to them, the more you'll receive and recognise.

When I first met my spirit guides, I was like, "Hey, what's up?" And they were like, "Oh, just here to hang out and help you on your spiritual journey, babe." And I was like, "Cool, cool." And ever since then, they've been my go-to for all things spiritual.

That was not at all how it happened. I met a whole bunch of mine during reiki sessions and it was so amazing in the ways they showed up. I believe I met so many of them at the time because it was one of the first times that I've gone into the fifth dimension and also because one of my sessions became about clearing and entity attachment, I believe that they showed up to help and protect me. Here are some of my spirit guides:

Solomon, the black panther: is one of my cherished spirit guides. Despite his advanced age and regal demeanour, he possesses a distinct personality from mine. In the past, Solomon served as my negative entity attachment. However, after purging the negative energy, he reappeared as a panther and has been my constant companion for several years. Although I have the ability to summon him whenever I desire, our initial encounter was quite surreal. He was with me from four years old and I think that we've had some very strong attachments in our previous lives. I have asked him about those previous lives, but I will.

I got a little surprise when I opened up my Akashic records. These two gods and goddesses from Egypt stepped right on in, and let me tell you, it was a shock. I didn't even know who they were at first, but once I found out, it made total sense.

These Egyptian deities came through to offer me some much-needed protection, and let me tell you, I was grateful. I'll spill the tea on what Akashic records are later, but just know that when these gods and goddesses step in, you better pay attention. They know what you need, even if you don't. So, if you're feeling like you need some protection in your life, call upon the gods and goddesses of Egypt. They've got your back.

Sekhmet: Sekhmet is known for being the goddess of war, healing, and hunting. You don't want to mess with her, 'cause she'll bring the heat. She's not only fierce but she's got the power to protect and heal. Plus, her name literally means "powerful one," and trust me, she lives up to it.

So, if you're feeling like you need some warrior energy in your life, call upon Sekhmet. She'll give you the strength and protection you need to conquer whatever life throws your way. Just don't forget to show her the respect she deserves, or else you might just get on her bad side.

Sorbek: This dude is a straight-up boss, with the head of a crocodile and the body of a man. And let me tell you, he's not someone you want to cross.

Sobek is known as the god of the Nile and fertility. He's got the power to bring abundance and prosperity into your life, but he won't hesitate to take it away if you disrespect him. So, make sure you show him the respect he deserves, or else you'll feel the wrath of his crocodile jaws.

But don't let his tough exterior fool you. Sobek is also known for his nurturing side. He's got the power to protect and provide for his followers, kind of like a crocodile momma protecting her babies. So, if you're in need of some abundance and protection in your life, call upon Sorbek.

Kwame: He's an African warrior, and he came just in time before I had to deal with this negative entity. He said he was there to protect me and we go way back - hundreds of years back, to be exact. Since we removed that negative entity a few years ago, I haven't really connected with him as much. But let me tell you, when that entity attacked me, he was there, ready to fight alongside me. I'm forever grateful for Kwame and his warrior spirit.

Rosetta: she's an old woman in a rocking chair, looking all wise and experienced. But the catch? She doesn't speak English and I don't speak her language. So, like, what's the point, right? I didn't really feel a connection with her, which is weird 'cause I thought I was supposed to feel all connected to my spirit guides. But hey, it just goes to show that you can be selective about who you take advice from and who you actually connect with. Don't settle for someone just 'cause they're a spirit guide, you deserve the best.

Others: Not only have I seen a freaking unicorn (yeah, they're real, hun), but I've also had an eagle pop up multiple times, and this brown moth butterfly thing - I don't even know what it is, but it's there. And here's the kicker, I haven't even bothered to really connect with them, which is such a shame. I need to get my act together and tap into these spirit guides, 'cause if I've learned anything, it's that they're here for a reason. Time to start building some bridges and making some spirit connections, y'all.

But let's get real, meeting your spirit guides is not always easy. Sometimes you gotta do some serious soul-searching and meditation to make that connection. And not all guides are created equal - you gotta be discerning and make sure you're connecting with the right ones.

But if you do, it's like having a spiritual dream team on your side. They've got your back and are always ready to help you navigate life's twists and turns. So don't be afraid to reach out and make that connection - your spirit guides are waiting for you.

To make the most of your squad's assistance, you have to be aware of their existence and ask for their help. As a psychic, I help clients identify who's who on their squad, but if you're not sure, don't sweat it. Just address them as a whole in your thoughts, meditations or journal. And here's a rundown of some of the main positions on your team:

Your spirit guides, they want to talk to you and they'll do it any way they can. They might send you signs, you know, those synchronistic moments that Carl Jung was always talking about. Like, you're having a fight with your partner and then the next day, you see a book about communication in romantic relationships just sitting on a co-worker's desk.

They might talk to you through numbers, like seeing 111 everywhere, or your lucky number showing up in unexpected places. They might even send you a message through music, like that one song that always lifts you up playing on the radio when you're having a bad day.

Here are some ways to chat to them:

1. You can't expect to have a conversation with your spirit guides if you're all frazzled and stressed out. Take some time to relax, meditate, or do some yoga to get in the right headspace.
2. Ask for their help. , they can't read your mind, you gotta ask for their help. Say it out loud or write it in a journal, but make sure you're specific about what you need help with.
3. Keep your eyes and ears open. Your spirit guides

might be trying to communicate with you, but you gotta be paying attention. Look out for synchronicities, numbers, or messages in your dreams.

4. Show gratitude. You gotta show your spirit guides some love and appreciation. Offer them some gratitude and leave them some offerings, like candles, flowers or crystals.

5. Get to know them. Your spirit guides have their own personalities, interests and their own way of communicating. Take some time to get to know them, and you'll be able to communicate with them more effectively.

And don't even get me started on dreams, spirit guides love to talk to us through our dreams. They might give you an idea on how to handle a situation, or they might even appear to you in a dream. So, stay alert and keep your eyes and ears open, cuz your spirit guides are trying to communicate with you.

I am truly grateful to have my spirit team by my side. There was a time when I felt so alone, but now I feel like I am constantly surrounded by these higher beings. I can always turn to them for advice, and because their guidance comes from the fifth dimension, it's always on point and never leads me astray.

What's even better is that they never interfere with my life unless I want them to. It's like having a personal team of advisers that you can call upon whenever you need them. If you're feeling lost or alone, I highly recommend calling upon your spirit team. They will have your back and make you feel supported. Trust me, it's one of the best things you can do for yourself.

ANGELS:

I never thought I would believe in the existence of angels. Growing up, my belief in them was solely shaped by Christianity. However, at the age of 14, I began to question my beliefs and ultimately stopped believing in them. It wasn't until I started training in Reiki that I had my first encounter with angel energy. During my training, I learned symbols and techniques to channel healing energy. It was through this process that I saw glowing angel wings, which I instinctively knew were real due to the way I felt.

I trust my feelings as a compass to guide me in life and seeing the angel wings only confirmed this. It was my attunement to Reiki that allowed me to finally experience angels with my third eye. Now, I mainly work with Angel Michael, but also receive messages from Gabriel and Metatron. As I continue to do spiritual work, I understand that the purpose is to help others heal and connect to themselves. This work is a message from the universe or God to be a messenger and share content that can help others. I'm still exploring my connection with different angels, but I look forward to working more with Gabriel and expanding my spiritual journey.

Ready to up your angel game? �� Let's dive into the divine world of celestial beings, shall we? From Guardian Angels to Archangels, each type of angel has its own unique personality & purpose.

Let's start with Metatron. Angel Metatron, also known as the "Voice of God," is a powerful and beloved angel in many spiritual traditions. He is often considered the highest of all angels, and is said to be the one who transcribes God's words and passes them along to humanity. But despite his lofty reputation, Metatron is also known for being approachable and accessible to those who seek his guidance and assistance.

So how can you work with Angel Metatron? One common way is to simply call on him by name and ask for his help or guidance. Some people find it helpful to light a candle or burn incense as they call on him, while others prefer to meditate or do visualization exercises in order to connect with him more deeply. You can also keep his energy close by carrying a talisman or other symbol of his presence, or by surrounding yourself with other objects that help you feel connected to his energy.

At the end of the day, the most important thing is to approach your relationship with Angel Metatron with an open heart and a willingness to receive his guidance. Whether you're looking for help with a specific problem, seeking spiritual growth and enlightenment, or simply looking for a deeper connection with the divine, this powerful angel is a wonderful resource and ally to have by your side. So go ahead and reach out to him today – you never know what kind of magic might come your way!

Guardian angels: Next, we've got our trusty Guardian Angels. Think of them as your personal bodyguards, always by your side to guide and protect you. These guys are always on call, 24/7, no breaks, no vacation days. Lucky for us, they never need a sick day.

I love working with angels, I feel so protected and I often have conversations with them. In particular and best but with Michael, you can read about. He's a very strong presence and has like this warrior energy to him which I love. And I often call upon Gabriel, who can seem somewhat harsh sometimes but I also really enjoy channelling them and getting my next steps on certain things that I need to know, hear or feel.

And don't even get me started on the names. They sound like they were ripped straight out of a superhero movie! The names alone are enough to make you feel like you're part of an exclusive club. Michael, Gabriel, Raphael, Uriel, Azrael, Jophiel, and Chamuel - these names roll off the tongue like a battle cry.

Next, we've got the big dogs, the Archangels. These guys are the VIPs of the angelic world and bring some serious power to the table. From Gabriel, the messenger of God, to Michael, the protector, these angels bring divine guidance and strength to those who call upon them.

And last but certainly not least, we've got the adorable little Cherubs. These chubby-cheeked cuties bring joy and happiness wherever they go. So, if you're feeling down, just call on a Cherub for a pick-me-up!

If you're looking for a celestial BFF who's got your back, then look no further than Angel Michael! This guy is the ultimate wingman, known for being the protector and defender of the faith. He's like the superhero of the angel world, ready to save the day and make sure you're never feeling lonely.

So what makes Angel Michael so special? For starters, he's one of the Archangels, which means he's got some serious street cred in the angel world. He's also associated with courage, strength, and protection, making him the go-to guy when you need a little extra support. Whether you're facing a tough decision, feeling overwhelmed, or just need a confidence boost, Angel Michael is always there to lend a helping hand.

If you're looking to work with Angel Michael, there are a few ways to do it. You can call upon him for guidance and protection through prayer or meditation. You can also ask him to help you overcome fears, achieve your goals, and find the courage to follow your dreams. Whether you're feeling lost or just need a little extra encouragement, Angel Michael is always there to help.

Angel Gabriel is the ultimate wingman (or wing-angel, if you will) in the spiritual world. This celestial being is known for being the messenger of God, delivering important messages and guidance to individuals on their life journey. But don't let the "delivery boy" reputation fool you, Gabriel is a force to be reckoned with.

Think of Gabriel as your personal hype-angel, always there to give you the boost of confidence you need to take on the world. This angel is known for helping individuals with communication, creativity, and self-expression. If you're feeling like your words are falling on deaf ears or like you just can't seem to get your ideas across, call on Gabriel for some celestial communication support.

Not only is Gabriel great for helping with self-expression, but they're also known for being a guardian angel to pregnant women, providing guidance and protection during pregnancy and childbirth. So, if you or a loved one are expecting, don't hesitate to call on Gabriel for some extra support.

Gabriel is the ultimate spirit guide for communication and self-expression, always there to give you a boost of confidence and support you on your life journey. So, don't be afraid to call on this celestial wingman for some divine guidance and support.

Raphael is often referred to as the "Healing Angel," as his main role is to bring physical, emotional, and spiritual healing to those in need. He's often depicted holding a staff or carrying a bottle of medicine, symbolizing his power to heal and restore balance to those he interacts with.

But don't let the "healing" label fool you, Raphael is a total badass. He's not just a soft, gentle nurse - he's a fierce warrior when it comes to protecting and guiding his charges. He's got a bold, adventurous spirit and is always ready for a challenge, making him the perfect companion for those who are feeling stuck or uncertain about their next steps in life.

So, if you're looking to work with Raphael, don't be afraid to get a little wild! Ask him to be your guide on a new adventure, or call upon him when you're feeling lost or in need of healing.

Angel Uriel is known as the "Angel of Wisdom" and is said to help guide people towards a path of knowledge and understanding. This powerful angel is also associated with creativity, inspiration, and communication. When working with Uriel, you may feel a sense of clarity and enlightenment, as he helps to bring clarity to complex situations and helps you to make sense of the world around you.

To work with Uriel, it's important to cultivate a love of learning and knowledge. Read books, attend workshops and seminars, and engage in intellectual pursuits that will help you grow and expand your understanding of the world. Additionally, try to tap into your own creativity by exploring new interests and engaging in activities that bring you joy and inspiration.

When communicating with Uriel, be open and receptive to the messages he may have for you. Some people find it helpful to meditate or perform a simple ritual to help connect with this powerful angel. You may also choose to keep a journal and write down any insights or messages you receive from Uriel, as this can help you to stay focused on your path and deepen your connection with him over time.

Angel Azrael is often known as the "Angel of Death," but that's just one aspect of this multifaceted angelic being. Azrael is responsible for guiding souls through the transition from life to the afterlife and helping to ease the process of letting go.

But, don't get too spooked by Azrael's reputation! This angel is also known for offering comfort and support in times of grief and loss. Azrael is a powerful ally for those who are grieving, and can help to bring peace and closure to those who are struggling.

To work with Angel Azrael, start by setting an intention to connect with this angelic being. You can do this through meditation, visualization, or simply speaking to Azrael out loud. Call upon Azrael's support during times of grief, and ask for guidance and comfort in your journey. Trust that Azrael is always with you, even in the face of loss, and let go of any fears or anxieties you may have about death. Azrael is a gentle and loving angel, who is always there to help you through even the toughest transitions.

Angel Jophiel, also known as the "Angel of Wisdom" is a celestial being who embodies divine wisdom, enlightenment, and beauty. Jophiel is believed to help individuals tap into their inner wisdom and see the beauty in all things. Working with Angel Jophiel can bring peace and joy to your life, as well as help you make better decisions and find clarity in your thoughts and actions.

So, how can you work with Angel Jophiel? One way is to call upon him when you need help making a decision or finding clarity in a situation. You can also call upon Jophiel to help you see the beauty in your life and find joy in even the simplest of things. Additionally, you can meditate on the color yellow, which is associated with Jophiel, to help you tap into his energy.

Remember, the most important thing when working with Angels, including Jophiel, is to have an open heart and mind. Angels are here to help us, but they will only do so if we invite them in and allow them to assist us. So, go ahead, have a chat with Jophiel and see how he can bring a little bit of divine wisdom and beauty into your life!

Here's how you can work with your guardian angels:

1. Ask and you shall receive. If you want to work with your guardian angels, you have to ask for their help.

Simply call out to them, whether it's through prayer, meditation, or simply speaking out loud, and let them know you're ready to work together.

2. Listen to your intuition. Your guardian angels are always communicating with you, but sometimes it can be difficult to hear them over the noise of the world. Pay attention to your gut feelings, dreams, and synchronicities, as these are often signs from your angels.

3. Practice gratitude. Angels love it when we show gratitude for the blessings in our lives. Take some time each day to give thanks for the people, experiences, and things that make you happy.

I start each day by calling on Archangel Michael for help. This powerful archangel is known for his ability to protect and guide those who call on him, so I always feel like I'm in good hands when I reach out.

One of the ways I connect with Archangel Michael is through automatic writing. This technique involves allowing the pen to move freely across the page without consciously controlling it, and can be a powerful tool for receiving guidance and messages from the spiritual realm.

When I sit down to do automatic writing, I begin by setting the intention to connect with Archangel Michael. I'll ask for his guidance, protection, and support, and then let the pen do its thing. I always find that the messages I receive through automatic writing are powerful and profound, and often offer insights and wisdom that I wouldn't have been able to access on my own.

Angel numbers:

Your guides can communicate with you in many ways, and it isn't just angels that use numbers to communicate with you. This is all part of numerology. Numerology is like the secret language of the universe, and it's been around for centuries. It's all about the energy, intention, and vibration behind numbers and letters. In short, it's like the universe's own shorthand, and each number holds a specific meaning. There are different ways to interpret numerology, like the Pythagorean system and the Chaldean method, but they all aim to decipher the hidden messages. And guess what, other spiritual fields like palm reading and astrology also borrow from numerology. It's like the backbone of all things mystical, your astrological sign is based on your birth date, and your enneagram type is based on a number, from one to nine. So, be open to the power of numbers, and you'll be surprised at how much they can reveal about you. We're going to go into this further, but first let's talk about how angels and guides use numbers to communicate with you.

Angel numbers are a way for the universe to communicate with us through numbers. You may see certain number sequences repeatedly, like 111 or 444, and that's the universe trying to send you a message. These numbers can hold special meanings or be a sign of guidance from your angels. The next time you see a number sequence popping up everywhere, pay attention, it could be the universe trying to drop some knowledge on you.

Seeing your angel number once is cool, but seeing it twice is like "oh, the universe is trying to tell me something" and seeing it three times in a row, well that's a whole other level of "HEY, PAY ATTENTION." Trust me, the more you see it, the more powerful the message is. So, next time you see that number sequence popping up everywhere, don't just brush it off, it could be the universe giving you a little nudge, a sign of empowerment, a confirmation that you are in the flow and aligned with the universe. So, be open to new opportunities, put yourself out there and trust that the universe has got your back.

So, don't just brush it off, read below and figure out what your angel numbers mean for you, and make sure to thank the universe for the heads up.

The angel number 111 is a powerful symbol that is often seen as a sign of manifestation. When you see this number sequence repeatedly, it may be a sign from the universe that your thoughts and desires are being aligned and manifested into reality. This number is also associated with new beginnings, so it may be an indication that a new chapter or phase of your life is about to begin.

In addition to manifestation and new beginnings, the number 111 is also associated with spiritual awakening and enlightenment. This number is often seen as a sign to pay attention to your thoughts, as they have a powerful impact on the reality you are creating. It is a reminder to stay positive and to trust in the journey and the universe's plan for you. Seeing 111 is a reminder to stay focused on your goals and to have faith that they will come to fruition.

The angel number 222 is a powerful symbol that is often seen as a sign of balance and harmony. When you see this number sequence repeatedly, it may be a sign from the universe that everything is aligning perfectly in your life. This number is also associated with partnerships, so it may be an indication that a new relationship or collaboration is about to begin. So, if you're single and ready to mingle, keep an eye out for 222, it could be a sign that your soulmate is on the way.

In addition to balance and harmony, the number 222 is also associated with trust and faith. This number is often seen as a sign to trust in yourself and the path that you are on. It's a reminder to have faith that everything will work out in your favor and that the universe has your back. Seeing 222 is a reminder that you are exactly where you are supposed to be, and to have confidence in your decisions.

The angel number 333 is a powerful symbol that is often seen as a sign of the Ascended Masters' presence and guidance in your life. When you see this number sequence repeatedly, it may be a sign from the universe that the Ascended Masters are working with you, helping you on your journey, and answering your prayers. This number is also associated with spiritual growth, so it may be an indication that you are on the right path and making progress on your spiritual journey.

In addition to the Ascended Masters' presence and spiritual growth, the number 333 is also associated with creativity and self-expression. This number is often seen as a sign to express yourself freely and to pursue your passions. It's a reminder to trust your intuition and to be true to yourself. Seeing 333 is a reminder that you are being supported in your creative endeavors, and to have confidence in your abilities. So, go forth and express yourself, sassy pants. The universe has got your back.

The angel number 444 is a powerful symbol that is often seen as a sign of the Archangels' presence and guidance in your life. When you see this number sequence repeatedly, it may be a sign from the universe that the Archangels are working with you, helping you on your journey, and answering your prayers. This number is also associated with inner wisdom and the guidance of your inner voice, so it may be an indication that you are on the right path and that your inner voice is leading you towards your goals.

In addition to the Archangels' presence and inner wisdom, the number 444 is also associated with stability and security. This number is often seen as a sign to have confidence in yourself and trust that everything will work out in your favour. It's a reminder to keep your feet on the ground and to be present in the moment. Seeing 444 is a reminder that you are in a safe and secure place and that the universe is supporting you in every way. So, trust in yourself and trust in the journey, the universe has got your back.

The angel number 555 is a powerful symbol that is often seen as a sign of major life changes and personal freedom. When you see this number sequence repeatedly, it may be a sign from the universe that big changes are on the horizon, and it's time to let go of the old and embrace the new. This number is also associated with personal freedom, so it may be an indication that you are being called to break free from any limiting beliefs or situations and to trust that everything will work out for the best.

In addition to major life changes and personal freedom, the number 555 is also associated with adventure and new opportunities. This number is often seen as a sign to take risks and to step out of your comfort zone. It's a reminder to be open to new experiences and to trust that the universe has something amazing planned for you. Seeing 555 is a reminder that you are on the right path and that it's time to take action towards your goals and dreams. So, don't be afraid of change, sass-a-lots, embrace it and make it work for you.

The angel number 666 is a powerful symbol that is often seen as a sign of balance and harmony in your material and financial aspects. When you see this number sequence repeatedly, it may be a sign from the universe that you are out of balance in some way, and it's time to take a closer look at your material and financial situation. This number is also associated with practicality and responsibility, so it may be an indication that you need to take a more responsible approach to your finances and trust that everything will work out for the best.

In addition to balance and harmony, the number 666 is also associated with problem-solving and overcoming obstacles. This number is often seen as a sign to focus on finding solutions and to be persistent in your efforts. It's a reminder to not give up and to trust that the universe will guide you in the right direction. Seeing 666 is a reminder that you are capable of overcoming any challenges that come your way and having confidence in your abilities. So, don't be afraid to face your financial challenges, you got this.

The angel number 777 is a powerful symbol that is often seen as a sign of good luck and fortune, both spiritually and materially. When you see this number sequence repeatedly, it may be a sign from the universe that you are on the right path and that good luck and blessings are headed your way. This number is also associated with spiritual awakening and development, so it may be an indication that you are making progress on your spiritual journey and to trust that everything will work out for the best.

In addition to good luck and fortune, the number 777 is also associated with spiritual guidance and encouragement. This number is often seen as a sign to trust in your intuition and to be open to receiving guidance from your angels and the universe. It's a reminder that you are never alone and to have faith in the journey. Seeing 777 is a reminder that you are on the right path, and that the universe is supporting you every step of the way. So, don't be afraid to trust your intuition and to have faith in the journey, the universe has got your back.

The angel number 888 is a powerful symbol that is often seen as a sign of abundance and prosperity, both spiritually and materially. When you see this number sequence repeatedly, it may be a sign from the universe that you are on the right path and that abundance and prosperity are headed your way. This number is also associated with personal authority and personal power, so it may be an indication that you are in a position of power and to trust that everything will work out for the best.

In addition to abundance and prosperity, the number 888 is also associated with the concept of karma and the law of cause and effect. This number is often seen as a sign to focus on your actions and to be mindful of the energy you are putting out into the world. It's a reminder that you are responsible for your own success and to have confidence in your abilities. Seeing 888 is a reminder that you are on the right path, and that the universe is supporting you every step of the way. So, be mindful of your actions, sass-a-doodle, and trust that the universe will reward you for your hard work.

The angel number 999 is a powerful symbol that is often seen as a sign of completion and the end of a phase or cycle in your life. When you see this number sequence repeatedly, it may be a sign from the universe that a certain aspect of your life is coming to an end and it's time to let go and move on. This number is also associated with the completion of a spiritual journey, so it may be an indication that you have reached a significant point in your spiritual development and trust that everything will work out for the best.

In addition to completion and endings, the number 999 is also associated with the concept of universal love and light. This number is often seen as a sign to focus on the positive aspects of life and to let go of the negative. It's a reminder that you are part of the universal energy, and to trust that the universe will guide you towards your goals. Seeing 999 is a reminder that you have reached the end of a certain phase in your life, and that the universe is supporting you every step of the way. So, let go of the past, and trust that the universe has something even better in store for you.

CHAPTER 5:
GUIDANCE FROM
THE UNIVERSE

Let me tell you something that's not so secret: The Universe is freaking amazing! It's like your personal genie, but instead of granting you three wishes, it's constantly sending you the answers and guidance that you need. Feeling lost or unsure? No problem! The Universe has your back.

So what is the Universe?

The universe is a vast and dynamic entity that encompasses all that we know and beyond. It is a manifestation of a force that is often referred to as the "creator energy," which is believed to have given birth to all that exists in the cosmos.

This creator energy is often associated with a divine or spiritual source that is beyond our physical understanding, and it is believed to be the driving force behind the creation of the universe, including the stars, planets, galaxies, and all living beings.

The concept of creator energy is the idea of a higher power or ultimate reality that transcends the limitations of the physical world. Energy is said to be present in all things and is the essence of everything that exists.

As I delved deeper into my spiritual journey, I came to the realisation that my intuition was not just a personal trait, but it was a force that was interconnected with the universe itself. The universe, which is often described as the "creator energy," is believed to have given birth to all that we know, from the tiniest particles to the largest galaxies.

For a long time, I struggled with the idea of a higher power. As a child, I went to a Christian school and was taught to believe in God as an all-powerful, judgmental figure who controlled everything in the universe. But as I grew older and began to question my faith, I realized that this version of God no longer resonated with me.

That's when I began to explore other spiritual practices and belief systems, and eventually came across the idea of the universe as a higher power. The universe is this vast, infinite, and interconnected web of energy that permeates everything and everyone. It's the force that gives life to all things and connects us to one another in ways that we may not fully understand.

At first, I was hesitant to call the universe "God" because of the negative connotations that word had for me. But as I delved deeper into my spiritual journey, I began to realize that "God" didn't have to mean what I thought it did. Instead, I could redefine the word to suit my own beliefs and experiences.

So I started calling the universe "God," not in the traditional Christian sense, but as a way of acknowledging the power and presence of something greater than myself. To me, God is no longer an external force that judges and punishes, but an internal one that connects me to the world around me and helps me to find meaning and purpose in my life.

Overall, I'm grateful for the journey that led me to the universe as my higher power, and for the freedom and peace that comes with letting go of the Christian version of what God meant for me. It's allowed me to embrace my spirituality on my own terms and to connect with something greater than myself in a way that feels authentic and true to who I am.

When it comes to my connection with God, I don't play by the traditional rules. I mean, who says God has to be all serious and stuffy? That's why I connect with a mischievous energy that has a wicked sense of humor.

I like to think of God as this playful spirit who's always ready to pull a prank or crack a joke. I mean, life is hard enough as it is, so why not lighten the mood a bit, right?

Sometimes I'll ask for guidance or support, and instead of a serious response, I'll get a pun or a one-liner that leaves me laughing my ass off. And you know what? It works. It helps me to feel more connected to the universe and reminds me that spirituality doesn't have to be boring or uptight.

So if you're looking for a fun and sassy way to connect with God, just follow my lead and embrace that mischievous energy. Who knows? You might just find that laughter is the best medicine after all.

God's got some serious desires, and they don't just involve lazing around on a cloud all day. No, no, no - God's main goal is to know and experience themselves in all their freaking glory. And let's be real, they're pretty darn glorious.

But here's the kicker - God's not selfish. They want every living being to know and experience their true selves, too. That's why they've given us all the power to create and shape our lives in any way we choose. It's called MANIFESTING.

And last but not least, God wants us to experience non-stop joy and fulfilment. Like, can you even imagine? Life is meant to be a never-ending journey of growth, expansion, and creation. Get ready to explore every nook and cranny of this wacky world.

Long story short, if we align ourselves with God's desires, we can unlock the full potential of our existence and live our best lives.

Moreover, the universe is in a constant state of expansion, as it follows the laws of physics. It is always growing and evolving, and while it may contract in the future, it is the natural order of things for the universe to expand. This constant expansion is a reflection of the universe's creative and life-giving force.

In the same way, our personal growth and development are tied to the natural order of expansion. We need to expand our knowledge, practice self-love, and contribute to the world around us to grow and evolve as individuals. Just like the universe, we have the potential to create and give life to new ideas, new relationships, and new experiences.

By tapping into our intuition and connecting with the universe's creator energy, we can open ourselves up to infinite possibilities and allow our lives to unfold in a way that is natural and aligned with our true purpose. We can trust that the universe has our back and is constantly working in our favour, even when we may not see the bigger picture.

So, let's embrace the natural order of expansion and growth, both in the universe and in our personal lives. Let's cultivate our intuition, connect with the creator's energy, and allow ourselves to expand and evolve in a way that is authentic and aligned with our true nature.

HOW CAN I WORK WITH THE UNIVERSE?

You can trust in something that's bigger than yourself and get all the answers that you need. It's like having a hotline to the divine. So, stop stressing about not knowing what to do and surrender to the magic of the Universe. It's like having a superpower that only a select few know how to use, and guess what? You're one of them. So, go forth and tap into that power!

By developing your presence and awareness you can connect with the universe and listen to its guidance. It's all about tapping into your intuition and recognising what's happening right now, which can lead you towards your path ahead. So, let's ditch the therapists and tune into the cosmic vibes for some much-needed direction! Think of it as a way to tap into your own intuition and start listening to the universe. Trust me, it's way cooler than just talking to yourself.

Asking for a sign is a power move. It means you're ready to let go of your control issues and work with the universe to get what you want. And if you don't get your sign, that's a sign too, so pay attention!

Asking for guidance is like a workout for your ability to receive good stuff from the universe. It's all about letting go of your expectations and trusting that the universe has a better plan than you do. And you can ask for a sign for anything you need, whether it's a big decision or just reassurance that you're on the right path. So, don't overthink it, just go with your gut and ask for the first sign that pops into your head.

There are more ways to connect with the universe than there are flavours at the ice cream parlour, so feel free to taste-test them all and see which one tickles your fancy. The real test is whether you're getting the answers you need, not necessarily the ones you want, and how it makes you feel. So, take your pick and let's get connected!

Here's the deal: you can't control the universe. No matter how hard you try to manipulate, bargain or beg, the universe is gonna do its own thing. So, if you really wanna get guidance from the universe, you need to surrender to it. That's right, let go of the control freak inside you and surrender to the unknown. Trust that the universe has a bigger, better plan for you than you could ever imagine. Because let's face it, your ego isn't always right. So, if you really want to get the best out of the universe, loosen your grip and surrender to the flow.

MEDITATION:

Practice quieting your mind and listening to your intuition during meditation. The universe often speaks to us in stillness and silence.

You know how everyone's always telling you to "just meditate" when you're feeling stressed or lost? Well, turns out they're onto something. Meditation is like a secret weapon for tapping into the universe's guidance. And it's not just about sitting cross-legged and chanting "ohm" (although, if that's your thing, go for it). It's about quieting your mind, tuning out the noise of the world around you, and getting in touch with your inner self. Whether you do it for five minutes or an hour, meditation is a way to open yourself up to the universe and receive the guidance you need. So, next time someone tells you to meditate, don't roll your eyes – embrace it and see where it takes you.

If you thought meditation was just about sitting cross-legged and humming "om," then you've got another thing coming. There are all sorts of ways to get your zen on, and it's all about finding what works for you.

First up, we've got mindfulness meditation. This is all about living in the moment and observing your thoughts without judgment. So grab a seat, close your eyes, and focus on your breath. Whenever your mind starts to wander, just reel it back in like a fish on a line. You got this.
Next, we've got loving-kindness meditation. This is all about spreading the love.
Visualize yourself sending love and kindness to yourself, your

friends, your enemies (if you have any), and eventually to all living beings. It's like a warm hug for your soul.

And for all my active babes out there, we've got movement meditation. This is all about getting your body moving and finding your zen through motion. You can try yoga, dance, or even just a simple walk in nature. Let your body do the talking and your mind will follow.

So there you have it, boo. Meditation isn't just for monks and hippies. It's for anyone who wants to find their inner peace and get their groove on at the same time.

Not only does it help you find your inner peace, but it's also a great way to talk to the universe and get your daily dose of guidance and inspiration.

When I meditate, I like to think of it as my personal hotline to the universe. I can ask for whatever guidance or support I need, and the universe always delivers. It's like having a direct line to the cosmic source of all things. And let me tell you, it feels pretty good.

But that's not all, babe. Meditation is also a great way to work through problems and find solutions. When I'm feeling stuck or unsure about something, I'll sit down and meditate on it. I'll focus on the problem and let my mind wander, trusting that the universe will provide the answers I need. And you know what? It usually does.

So if you're looking for a way to connect with the universe and get your daily dose of inspiration, look no further than meditation, darling. It's like a one-stop-shop for all your spiritual needs.

PAY ATTENTION TO SIGNS AND SYNCHRONICITIES:

The universe communicates with us in many ways, but one of the most common is through signs and synchronicities. These are events or coincidences that seem to have a deeper meaning or significance. For example, you might see the same number or symbol repeatedly, or you might have a sudden urge to do something that leads you to a chance encounter or opportunity. These signs can often guide us on our path, so it's important to pay attention and trust your intuition.

To help recognise these signs, try keeping a journal or note on your phone of any notable coincidences or patterns that catch your attention. Reflect on their potential meaning, and see if there is any guidance or message the universe may be trying to send you. It's important to trust your intuition and follow any inner guidance that may come from these signs, as they can often lead us to unexpected but fulfilling paths. Remember, the universe has our back, and is always providing guidance and support for those who are open to it.

DREAMS:

The universe can speak to us through our dreams. Keep a dream journal and reflect on the messages that may be hidden in your dreams.

You know, those wild adventures your mind takes you on while you're catching some Z's? Well, turns out they're not just random gibberish. Your dreams can actually be a powerful tool for tapping into the universe and receiving guidance. So, next time you wake up from a crazy dream, don't just shrug it off as nonsense. Take a closer look and see what messages the universe might be sending you. And hey, if nothing else, at least you got to have some fun in dreamland, right?

INTUITION

Trust your gut feelings and listen to your inner voice. The universe often speaks to us through our intuition.

It's like your inner GPS system that helps you navigate life. You know when you get a gut feeling or a hunch about something? That's your intuition talking to you. It's that little voice in your head that says "uh uh, don't do it" or "yes girl, go for it".

But here's the thing, sometimes we don't trust our intuition because we're too busy listening to other people or our logical brain. But let me tell you, your intuition knows what's up. It's connected to the universe and can guide you towards what's best for you.

So, if you're feeling lost or unsure about a decision, close your eyes and listen to your intuition. It might just surprise you with some real talk that you need to hear. Trust me , your intuition has got your back.

VISUALISATION:

Use visualisation techniques to connect with the universe and manifest your desires. Visualise yourself already having what you want and trust that the universe will bring it to you.

Visualisation is like creating your own personal movie! It's like daydreaming with a purpose, where you manifest your desires and bring them to life. When you visualise, you use the power of your imagination to create a mental image of what you want to achieve or experience, and the universe takes note. It's like creating a vision board in your mind, and the more detailed and vivid your visualisation is, the more powerful it becomes. You can visualise anything from attracting abundance, to healing relationships, to manifesting your dream job.

But here's the catch, babe, you can't just visualise and then sit on your couch all day waiting for it to happen. You've got to take inspired action towards your vision, and the universe will conspire to make it happen. Visualisation is like a GPS that guides you towards your destination, but you still have to drive the car. So, if you want to use visualisation to manifest your desires, start by setting a clear intention, creating a mental image of your desired outcome, and feeling the emotions that come with it. And then, take inspired action towards your vision, and trust that the universe will guide you towards your desired destination.

This is how I got the universe to spill the tea. I simply asked the universe to show me the way to my highest self, or to give me some answers to questions that were bugging me. And voila, the universe would send me a random vision, like a person walking on the beach, or a damn badger. And then I would dive deep into the spiritual meaning of those visions. It's like receiving a message from the universe in a really trippy and cool way.

One thing that really gets my clients in touch with the universe is when I ask them to set an intention and then we work on a visualization exercise together. It's like tapping into your own imagination, but with the purpose of seeking guidance from the universe. I ask them to close their eyes and imagine themselves in a particular setting or scenario, and then I guide them through a series of prompts to get more specific about what they see, hear, and feel. Then we go over the meaning of the vision and how it relates to their intention. It's a really powerful and accurate way to get what they need.

PRAYER:

Ask the universe for guidance through prayer. Trust that your prayers will be answered in the way that is best for you.

That's where prayer comes in. It's like a conversation with a higher power. You put your thoughts and intentions out there and let the universe respond. It's a powerful way to connect to the universe and get the guidance you need. And don't worry, you don't have to be religious to pray. It's all about setting your intentions and having faith in the universe. So, next time you're feeling lost or in need of guidance, take a moment to pray and see what the universe has in store for you.

Here's a prayer you can use to ask for guidance from the universe:

Dear universe,

I come to you with an open heart and mind, seeking your guidance and wisdom.

Please show me the way to my highest good, and guide me towards my purpose in life.

Help me to trust my intuition and recognise the signs you send me, so that I may make the best decisions for myself and those around me.

I am open to receiving your messages in any form they may come, and I trust that you will always lead me towards love, light, and abundance.

Thank you for your constant presence and guidance in my life.

Amen.

How I talk to beings:

Automatic writing:

Here's how it works: you sit down with a pen and paper, clear your mind, and let the words flow. You don't think too hard about what you're writing, you just let it come out naturally. It's like a game of word association where the words on the page may not make sense at first, but as you keep going, a message or idea starts to form.

When it comes to automatic writing, you don't need to worry about being the next Shakespeare or stressing over spelling and grammar. None of that matters, got it? What really counts is tuning into your intuition and setting your heart-centred intentions. So let go of any fears of not being a "good writer" and just let the words flow from your soul!

Automatic writing, also known as psychography, is like tapping into a secret vault of wisdom inside of you that even you didn't know existed! It's all about going into a trance-like state and letting your pen hit the paper without any conscious thought. Don't worry about trying to be "in the zone" or achieving some kind of fancy meditative state - just let your inner badass take over and do the talking!

When you let go of your inner control freak and allow the words to flow without any judgment, you tap into a deep well of wisdom within yourself that you didn't even know existed. It's like having a hotline to your soul, where you can receive guidance, clarity, and insight on any topic that's been on your mind. And the best part? You don't have to rely on anyone else to give you the answers, because you have them all within you. So say goodbye to self-doubt, confusion, and indecision, and hello to your own personal source of enlightenment. Automatic writing is like having your own personal guru at your fingertips! You can use it for ANYTHING.

Automatic writing is the secret sauce that many spiritual seekers crave for a little spice in their lives. It's like adding a dash of mystery and magic that can make your spiritual journey feel both humbling and healing.

It's not just some trendy hobby, either. Automatic writing is a legit spiritual practice that can be just as powerful as doing yoga or meditating. Why? Because it's a direct path to self-realization and spiritual Oneness, connecting you to the Divine like nobody's business.

And let me tell you when you tap into that Divine connection through automatic writing, you're in for some major guidance, direction, and insight. It's like having your very own spiritual GPS to guide you to your true Home.

When I'm asking for guidance from any of my spirit guides, or the Arcturians, I ask questions such as what do I need to know today? What is the message that benefits the collective to live the highest timeline? It might be how do I find my way towards my purpose today or what steps shall I take today?

You can do automatic writing anytime, anywhere! Whether you're feeling overwhelmed and need some guidance, or you just want to connect with your inner wisdom and intuition, automatic writing can be your go-to practice. It's perfect for those moments when you need to tap into your deeper knowing or access the mysterious realms beyond our everyday awareness. So, whether you're sitting at your desk or lounging on your couch, grab a pen and paper, get into a relaxed state, and let the magic flow!

CHANNELLING:

This one is my FAVE. When you channel, you're tuning into a higher consciousness or a specific entity, and then allowing their messages to flow through you like a vessel. It's like becoming a conduit for higher knowledge and spiritual guidance. Think of it as being a messenger for the Universe, only without the snail mail and postage stamps.

Channeling is a personal and unique experience, just like your taste in music or fashion sense. Some people might hear messages clairaudiently, while others might see visions or receive downloads of information. It's all about finding what works for you and learning to trust your intuition. So, my advice would be to start by setting a clear intention and creating a sacred space to work in. Then, try different techniques like meditation, automatic writing, or energy healing to help you connect with the spirit world. And most importantly, be patient with yourself and trust that the right spirits or beings will come through when the time is right.

Just as I went into channelling in the chapter all about your different Claire gifts, this is a really great way to connect to intergalactic beings.

It's important to be cautious and avoid using tools like an Ouija board if you aren't properly trained or experienced in doing so. These tools can potentially open up doors to unwanted energies or entities, and without proper knowledge and precautions, it can be difficult to protect yourself from any negative consequences that may arise.

Always create protection around you before you channel. You can use this:

"Universe, I call upon your protection and guidance. I ask that you surround me with your loving and healing light, and that you shield me from any negative energies, entities, or influences. I invoke the power of the elements, the spirits of the earth, air, fire, and water, to join me in this circle of protection. May the earth ground me, the air clear my mind, the fire purify my soul, and the water cleanse my emotions.

I ask that you bless my craft and my intentions, and that you guide me in the use of my powers for the highest good of all. May my spells and rituals be infused with your divine light and wisdom, and may they bring healing, love, and harmony to myself and to those around me. I thank you for your protection and your presence, and I trust in your divine guidance. So mote it be."

TAROT AND ORACLE CARDS:

Use divination tools like tarot and oracle cards to tap into the guidance of the universe. Trust the messages that come through the cards and use them as a tool for self-reflection and growth.

Tarot is not just a bunch of pretty pictures with random meanings. It's a powerful tool that can help you connect with your intuition and gain insight into your life.

Now, there are 78 cards in a tarot deck, and each one has a unique meaning. But don't freak out, you don't have to memorize them all (unless you want to, of course). The best way to get started is to choose a deck that resonates with you, and then start practicing with the cards.

To do a reading, you'll need to shuffle the cards and ask a question. Then, you'll draw cards and interpret their meanings based on the question you asked. Simple, right? Well, not really. There are a lot of nuances and intricacies to tarot, but don't worry - you'll get the hang of it with practice.

And here's a little secret - you don't have to be a psychic or a witch to use tarot. Anyone can do it, as long as you're open to the experience and willing to trust your intuition. Plus, it's a fun and creative way to explore your inner world and gain insights into your life. So go ahead, grab a deck and start shuffling. The universe is waiting to speak to you!

If you're feeling a little lost and need some guidance, tarot spreads can be a powerful tool for tapping into the universe's wisdom. Each spread has its own unique focus and can help you explore different aspects of your life, from love and relationships to career and personal growth. With a little practice and an open mind, you'll be interpreting tarot cards like a pro in no time. So, buckle up and get ready to connect with the universe in a whole new way!

1. The Past-Present-Future Spread: This is a classic spread that gives you an idea of what's happened, what's happening now, and what's to come. It's like a timeline of your life, but with some extra woo-woo goodness.

2. The Cross Spread: This spread will give you a deeper understanding of a specific situation or question. It involves drawing cards in a cross shape, with each card representing different aspects of the situation. Think of it as a more in-depth look at a specific topic.

3. The Relationship Spread: This spread is all about your connections with others. It can be used for romantic relationships, friendships, or even work relationships. It can help you understand what's going on beneath the surface and how to improve the connection.

4. The Celtic Cross Spread: This is the mother of all spreads . It's a complex spread that gives you a deep dive into a situation, with ten cards representing different aspects of the situation. It's not for the faint of heart, but it can be a game-changer when it comes to getting guidance from the universe.

5. The Yes/No Spread: This is a quick and dirty spread that gives you a simple answer to a yes or no question. It involves drawing a single card, with upright meaning yes and reversed meaning no. It's not the most in-depth spread, but it can be a helpful

tool for quick answers.

Oracle cards. These babies are like tarot cards' stylish and modern cousin. They are a tool to connect with the Universe and get guidance on your questions or concerns. There's more structure to tarot cards, whereas Oracle cards have a looser meaning and it's more for your own definition and intuition.

First things first, pick a deck that resonates with you. There are so many cool and funky designs out there, so find one that speaks to your soul.

Now, there are different types of Oracle cards. Some are all about angels and spirituality, others focus on affirmations and personal growth, and some are just straight-up weird and wonderful.

One of the most popular ways to use Oracle cards is to draw a daily card. Simply shuffle the deck and pick a card that jumps out at you. This card will offer you guidance or a message for your day.

I'm a big fan of Rebecca Campbell's decks, which are GORGEOUS and illustrated by the talented Danielle Noel.

How to do an oracle card reading:

1. First things first, you gotta clear your mind. Can't have any distractions or negative juju clouding your intuition. Find a quiet spot where you can really tune in to your inner self. And if you're reading for someone else, try to channel their vibes as you shuffle the cards.
2. Now, let's talk about shuffling. You can do it however you like, whether that's shuffling until a card dramatically jumps out at you, or stopping when you feel the moment is right. It's all about what feels good to you, baby.
3. When you're ready to draw your cards, ask your

intuition how many to pull. It could be one, it could be ten. It's up to you and your space constraints. Once you've got your cards, lay them face down and turn them over one by one.

4. And here's the most important part, trust your gut. What do those cards make you feel? What are your initial thoughts? Sometimes the most profound insights come from unexpected places, so keep an open mind. And if a card doesn't speak to you right away, take a few deep breaths and let your intuition do its thang.

Don't be afraid to trust your gut when reading those cards. As you get more comfortable with your deck, you'll find that the guidebook is more like a suggestion than a rulebook. You'll start to feel the energy of the cards and know what they're trying to tell you before you even turn to the book. So don't be shy about putting your own spin on things and trusting yourself more.

NUMEROLOGY:

The universe is always talking to you, and it's using numbers to do it. Your birthday, your name, your age, your address, your phone number, and your paycheck, are all made up of numbers. They're everywhere, and they're a part of you. The most straightforward way to understand how these numbers affect you is through your own personal numerology chart. This chart contains your life path number, among other core numbers, and it's based on your birthdate and full name. These numbers influence you in very personal ways, it's like the universe is speaking directly to you through numbers. So, pay attention to the numbers around you and within you, they might just hold the key to understanding yourself better.

The reason why I like it, is because even though it might seem that there are a lot of different methodologies for understanding yourself and getting closer to who you are which really is the point of all of this, numerology is very specific to you because it's based on the numerical make up of the time you were born and the day that you were born and there's a few different ways to work with it. And I've only seen quite a lot of accuracy with it.

Numerology works in a few ways, and every person goes through their own years from a sequence of 1 to 9, from when we are born and each year has its own meaning. Your Personal Year is like a year-long party, starting on your birthday and lasting until the next one. It's like a sneak peek into the events and opportunities that are coming your way. And let me tell you, it's a wild ride! We're talking 1, 2, 3, all the way up to 9, and then we start all over again.

Life is all about cycles, and we're no exception. Numerology has got us covered with 9 stages of development that we gotta go through as we grow and mature. Think of it as a journey, where we keep running into the same themes, just in different ways. But no matter what happens, the underlying principle remains the same.

Each number, from 1 to 9, has its own set of characteristics that tend to symbolise the 9 stages of the human life cycle. We're constantly incorporating these cycles into our lives, and it's a never-ending process. So grab your party hat, and let's see what the next Personal Year has in store for us! There are so many websites where you can find out what year you're on by putting your date of birth, so just look up 'personal year calculator numerology', and you'll quickly find something to help you.

Each year is like a different party, and each one has its own theme. So, let's break it down and see what each number has in store for us.

1 - The year of new beginnings! This is your time to shine! You're starting a new cycle, and it's time to make some big changes in your life. You'll feel a sense of independence and freedom, and you'll be ready to take on the world.

2 - The year of relationships and partnerships. This is the time to focus on your connections with others, whether it's romantic, friendships, or business. You'll be feeling more emotional and sensitive, so make sure to surround yourself with positive people.

3 - The year of creativity and self-expression. This is your time to let your artistic side shine! You'll be feeling more inspired and motivated than ever before, so don't be afraid to take risks and try new things

4 - The year of hard work and stability. This is the time to focus on building a solid foundation for your future. You'll be feeling more practical and organised, and you'll be ready to tackle any challenge that comes your way.

5 - The year of change and adventure. This is your time to break free from your routine and experience something new. You'll be feeling more spontaneous and carefree, so don't be afraid to try something new and exciting.

6 - The year of love and family. This is the time to focus on your relationships with loved ones, and to create a sense of harmony and balance in your life. You'll be feeling more nurturing and protective, and you'll be ready to take on the role of caretaker.

7 - The year of introspection and spiritual growth. This is the time to focus on your inner self and to explore your beliefs and values. You'll be feeling more introverted and contemplative, and you'll be ready to dig deep and discover your true self.

8 - The year of power and success. This is your time to take charge and make your dreams a reality. You'll be feeling more ambitious and confident, and you'll be ready to take on any challenge that comes your way.

9 - The year of completion and release. This is the time to let go of what no longer serves you and to make room for new beginnings. You'll be feeling more emotional and reflective, and you'll be ready to say goodbye to the past and welcome the future.

So there you have it! Each personal year has its own theme and energy, and it's up to you to make the most of it. Remember, life is a journey, and we're all constantly evolving and growing.

Life path numbers:

Let's talk about one of the most important numbers in

numerology, the life path number. This number is derived from your birthdate, and it represents your journey through life, your talents, and your goals. It's like your own personal GPS for your soul's journey.

Your life path number is the most important number in your numerology chart, it's like your destiny number. It's the sum of your birthdate and it gives an insight into your strengths, weaknesses, and tendencies. So, if you want to know what the universe has in store for you, and what kind of person you are, your life path number is the key.

If you wanna decode the universe's secret language, you gotta start with the basics. And when it comes to numerology, the basics are the single digits 1-9. These digits are the building blocks of every other number. You wanna know the meaning of any number? Just add up the digits and reduce it to a single digit. For instance, 17 is 8 because $1+7 = 8$, and 231 is 6 because $2+3+1 = 6$. By understanding the unique meanings of every single digit, you can then read the larger meaning of any other number. So, pay attention to the single digits, sass-a-frass, they hold the key to understanding the universe's hidden messages.

If you wanna know what the universe has in store for you and what kind of person you are, you gotta know your life path number. And, let me tell you, it's super easy to calculate. All you gotta do is take your birth date, add up the digits and reduce it to a single digit. Bam! That's your life path number.

For example, let's say your birthday is January 15, 1990. So, you add up the digits: $1+5+1+5+1+9+9+0 = 31$. Then, you reduce it to a single digit: $3+1 = 4$. So, your life path number is 4.

So, don't be afraid to do the math, sass-a-lot, your life path number holds the key to understanding yourself better, it's like a personal GPS for your soul's journey. And, trust me, knowing your life path number is worth the effort, it's like having a secret weapon to navigate through life with more grace and understanding.

So, if you want to know what the universe has in store for you, and what kind of person you are, your life path number is the key. It's like your own personal crystal ball, it gives you a glimpse into your journey through life and it helps you to understand yourself better. You can find your life path number by adding up the digits of your birthdate and reducing it to a single digit. So, don't be afraid to do the math, your life path number holds the key to understanding yourself better.

Number one:

If your life path number is 1, then you're a born leader and a trailblazer. You're independent and ambitious and you're not afraid to go against the grain. You're determined to make your mark on the world and you won't let anyone or anything stand in your way. You're a natural-born leader and you're not afraid to take charge, you're not afraid to be the first one to step up and take the initiative.

Being a life path 1 also means that you're a natural innovator, you're always looking for new ways to do things and you're not satisfied with the status quo. You're not afraid to take risks, and you're not afraid to fail. You're always looking for ways to improve and you're not afraid to challenge the status quo. You're a born leader and you're not afraid to blaze your own trail, sass-a-lot, so don't be afraid to be yourself, and don't be afraid to be a leader.

Number two:

If your life path number is 2, then you're a natural peacemaker and a diplomat. You're a sensitive and empathetic person, and you have a natural ability to sense the needs of others. You're a good listener and you're able to understand different perspectives. You're also a great mediator, and you're able to bring people together and resolve conflicts.

Being a life path 2 also means that you're a great team player and you're able to work well with others. You're able to bring out the best in people and to help them achieve their goals. You're a great collaborator, and you're able to bring different ideas and perspectives together to create something new and exciting. You're a natural peacemaker, sass-a-lot, and you're able to bring harmony and balance to any situation, so don't be afraid to use your natural ability to bring people together and to resolve conflicts.

Number three:

If your life path number is 3, then you're a natural-born creative, a self-expressionist and a social butterfly. You have a natural ability to communicate and to express yourself, whether it's through words, art, or music. You're a creative person and you have a great sense of humour, you're able to see the world in a different way and you're always looking for new ways to express yourself.

Being a life path 3 also means that you're a social person, you love to be around people and you enjoy making new friends. You have a great ability to connect with others and to make them feel at ease, you're a natural-born communicator, and you're able to express yourself in a way that others can understand. You're a creative person, sass-a-lot, and you're not afraid to express yourself, so don't be afraid to share your talents and to connect with others.

Number four:

if your life path number is 4, then you're a natural-born organiser and a hard worker. You're a practical person, and you have a great ability to plan and to organise. You're detail-oriented, and you're not afraid to roll up your sleeves and get to work. You're a person who values stability and security, you're a hard worker, and you're not afraid to put in the effort to achieve your goals

Being a life path 4 also means that you're a person who values discipline and responsibility, you're able to set realistic goals and to work steadily towards achieving them. You're a great problem-solver, and you're able to think strategically to overcome any obstacle. You're a hard worker, sass-a-lot, and you're not afraid to put in the effort to achieve your goals, so don't be afraid to be practical, responsible and to work hard to achieve your goals.

Number five:

If your life path number is 5, then you're a natural-born adventurer and a free spirit. You're a person who values freedom and independence, you're not afraid to take risks and to explore new things. You're a natural-born traveler, and you're always looking for new experiences and new ways to grow. You're a person who values change and diversity, you're adaptable and you're not afraid to explore the unknown.

Being a life path 5 also means that you're a person who values personal freedom and individuality, you're not afraid to be yourself and to be different. You're a creative person and you have a great ability to think outside the box. You're a natural-born adventurer, sass-a-lot, and you're not afraid to take risks, so don't be afraid to explore new things, to be yourself and to be different.

Number six:

if your life path number is 6, then you're a natural-born nurturer and a helper. You're a person who values love and harmony, you have a great ability to empathize with others and to put their needs before your own. You're a great listener and you're able to understand different perspectives. You're a natural-born peacemaker, and you're able to bring people together and to resolve conflicts.

Being a life path 6 also means that you're a person who values responsibility and duty, you're a great caregiver, and you're able to help others in a practical way. You're a responsible person and you're able to balance the needs of others with your own needs. You're a natural-born nurturer, sass-a-lot, and you're not afraid to help others, so don't be afraid to be a peacemaker and to help others in a practical way.

Number seven:

if your life path number is 7, then you're a natural-born seeker of knowledge and wisdom. You're a person who values understanding and the pursuit of knowledge, you have a great ability to think deeply and to analyze. You're a person who values solitude and you're able to find answers to life's mysteries through introspection. You're a natural-born thinker, and you're always looking for answers to the deeper questions of life.

Being a life path 7 also means that you're a person who values wisdom and spirituality, you have a great ability to understand the deeper meaning of things. You're a great problem solver, and you're able to think strategically to overcome any obstacle. You're a natural-born seeker, sass-a-lot, and you're not afraid to explore the deeper questions of life, so don't be afraid to seek knowledge and wisdom, to think deeply and to explore the deeper meaning of things.

Write about what the life path number 8 is in numerology in a sassy tone in two paragraphs

Listen up, sass-a-lot, if your life path number is 8, then you're a natural-born power player and a leader. You're a

Number eight:

if your life path number is 8, then you're a natural-born power player and a leader. You're a person who values ambition, success and material wealth. You have a great ability to manifest your goals and to turn your ideas into reality. You're a natural-born leader, and you're not afraid to take charge and to be in charge. You're a person who values power and influence, and you're not afraid to go after what you want.

Being a life path 8 also means that you're a person who values discipline, responsibility and hard work. You're able to set realistic goals and to work steadily towards achieving them. You're a great problem-solver, and you're able to think strategically to overcome any obstacle. You're a natural-born power player, sass-a-lot, and you're not afraid to go after what you want, so don't be afraid to be ambitious, to take charge and to be in charge.

Number nine:

if your life path number is 9, then you're a natural-born humanitarian and a philanthropist. You're a person who values compassion, kindness and selflessness. You have a great ability to empathize with others and to put their needs before your own. You're a person who values the greater good, and you're always looking for ways to help others and to make a difference in the world.

Being a life path 9 also means that you're a person who values selflessness and humility, you're able to put others' needs before your own. You're a great listener and you're able to understand different perspectives. You're a natural-born humanitarian, sass-a-lot, and you're not afraid to help others and to make a difference in the world, so don't be afraid to be compassionate, kind and to help others.

I never really used to be into numerology that much, and once I discovered that we each have our own life path number and we exhibit different qualities based on that, it started to interest me a lot more and I had the recommendation to use an app called Teledipity which I really enjoy and it basically gives you your monthly forecast and your yearly forecast based on your life path number and all my God if it isn't the most accurate thing I've ever read. So I would highly recommend downloading that.

If you're looking to connect with spirits or the universe, there are plenty of professionals out there who can help guide you. Psychics, mediums, and other spiritual practitioners have honed their skills to be able to communicate with the other side and can help you navigate that realm. Whether you're seeking guidance, clarity, or closure, they can provide insights and messages from beyond.

However, it's important to do your research and find a reputable practitioner who aligns with your beliefs and values. Not all psychics and mediums are created equal, and unfortunately, there are some who may not have your best interests at heart. Look for recommendations from trusted sources and read reviews to find someone who has a track record of providing helpful and ethical services.

And if you're not sure where to start, my app Woo Woo, can connect you with verified and vetted spiritual practitioners who can provide the guidance and support you're looking for.

CHAPTER 6: COMING BACK TO YOURSELF

The whole point of life isn't about making money, finding love, or achieving success. No, honey, it's all about coming back to yourself and remembering your self-worth.

You see, we live in a world that's constantly trying to tell us who we should be, how we should look, and what we should do. And it's easy to get caught up in all that noise and forget who we really are.

But here's the thing, boo. You are a badass, unique, and beautiful being, and you deserve to remember that. The whole point of life is to peel back all those layers of conditioning and societal expectations and get back to the core of who you are
.

It's about recognizing your own worth and value, and living your life in a way that honors that. Whether that means pursuing your passions, standing up for your beliefs, or simply taking time to love and care for yourself, it's all about coming back to that inner truth.

So don't let anyone tell you who you should be or what you should do. You are the boss of your own life, and the whole point of it all is to remember that and live it out loud.

A spiritual awakening is often about remembering who you are because throughout our lives, we tend to accumulate layers of conditioning, programming, and societal expectations that can obscure our true nature and purpose. We may find ourselves living someone else's idea of success or happiness, rather than following our own inner guidance.

During a spiritual awakening, we begin to peel back those layers and get back to the core of who we truly are. We may rediscover aspects of ourselves that we had forgotten or suppressed, and gain new insights into our purpose and meaning in life.

By remembering who we are, we can begin to live more authentically, in alignment with our true selves and our deepest values. This can bring a sense of liberation, joy, and fulfillment that we may not have experienced before.

Our subconscious mind starts forming when we're just little tykes, around seven years old. So, it's no surprise that our thoughts and emotions are mostly influenced by those around us, especially our parents or guardians. But once we grow up, it's time to break free from those preconceived notions and start shaping our own beliefs.

The power of the mind is no joke. Our thoughts and beliefs can shape our entire existence, for better or for worse. So, if something's not working for us, like a crappy job or a toxic relationship, it's time to take action and reparent ourselves.

If you want to live your best life, you need to start showing yourself some love and compassion. Reparenting is all about healing those emotional wounds from your childhood and developing a better relationship with yourself. You deserve it! But it's not just about feeling warm and fuzzy inside. Reparenting also means learning new skills, setting boundaries, and improving your communication game. By doing all of this, you'll be able to break those old negative patterns and build healthier relationships with yourself and the people around you.

So, let's talk about reparenting. It's all about being your own nurturing parent and healing those emotional wounds from your childhood. It's like giving yourself a big ol' hug and saying "I got you, boo." And hey, it's not always easy, but seeking help from a therapist or coach can be a game-changer. They can help you navigate the journey and give you the tools to succeed.

Now, why is reparenting important? Well, if you weren't parented in a healthy and supportive way, you might have some emotional wounds that need some TLC. And let's be real, those wounds can lead to negative patterns of behaviour and a distorted self-image. Nobody's got time for that, am I right? Reparenting gives you the chance to address those issues and develop a more positive and supportive relationship with yourself.

So, what does reparenting involve? It's all about developing a sense of self-compassion and self-acceptance, which can help you build a healthier sense of self-worth and improve your overall well-being. It also means learning new coping skills, setting boundaries, and developing more effective communication skills. By addressing these issues, you can break negative patterns of behaviour and build healthier relationships with yourself and others. So, if you're ready to break the cycle of self-sabotage and start living your best life, it's time to start reparenting.

Some of the specific benefits of reparenting can include:

1. Increased self-awareness: Reparenting helps individuals become more aware of their patterns of behaviour and the underlying emotions that drive them.
2. Improved self-esteem: By taking on the role of a nurturing parent, individuals can develop a more positive self-image and a greater sense of self-worth.
3. Greater self-compassion: Reparenting helps individuals learn to be kinder and more compassionate towards themselves, which can reduce negative self-talk and self-criticism.
4. Better coping skills: By addressing unresolved

emotional wounds from childhood, individuals can develop more effective coping skills to deal with stress and difficult situations.

5. Improved relationships: By developing a more positive and supportive relationship with oneself, individuals can improve their relationships with others, leading to healthier and more fulfilling connections.

It's all about coming back to love

What the soul really wants - it's the ultimate high of love that you can't even imagine. That's what it's after, That's the purpose of the soul, to get that feeling. It's not looking for knowledge, because knowledge is just a concept. It's the feeling that the soul is after, the experience of it all.

And you know what that feeling is? It's the feeling of being one with everything. It's like a big ol' bear hug from the universe, and that's what the soul craves. It's the ultimate truth that the soul yearns for, the perfect love that just makes you wanna dance around in your pajamas.

So let your soul feel it! Let it experience that pure, unadulterated love that comes with being at one with everything. Don't hold back, because that's what the soul is here for. To feel it all, and to know itself through those experiences.

At the core of our existence lies the fundamental truth that everything we do should come from a place of love. It's what drives us forward and keeps us connected to one another. But before we can spread that love out into the wider world, we first have to turn that love inward and learn to love ourselves fully and completely.

That's what coming back to the self is all about. It's about learning how to appreciate our own worth and to see ourselves in the best possible light. When we can love ourselves deeply, we create a powerful ripple effect that touches the lives of those around us. We become beacons of light that shine brightly and show others what is possible when we operate from a place of self-love.

In learning to love ourselves, we become more aware of our thoughts, feelings, and actions, and we start to see the beauty in all things. This newfound appreciation for ourselves spills over into the world around us, and we begin to see others in a more positive light.

The whole point of everything is to operate in love. When we love ourselves, we can extend that love to others, and it creates a ripple effect that can transform the world. Love is the very essence of our being, and it's up to us to nurture it, cultivate it, and share it with others.

So let's start by coming back to ourselves, by taking the time to appreciate who we are and all that we have to offer. Let's learn to love ourselves, to see ourselves in the best possible light, so that we can spread that love out into the world and make a positive impact on those around us. After all, love is the one thing that can truly change everything.

Coming to the feeling of love can be one of the most challenging things to do, especially when you're coming from a place of deep-seated trauma. It's a place where I once found myself, where my heart ached with a pain that I couldn't understand, and I was left with a sense of emptiness that seemed impossible to fill.

That's when I knew that something had to change. I had to find a way to break free from the cycle of pain and trauma that had been holding me back for so long. I had to find a way to connect with that elusive feeling of love, but it seemed like an impossible task.

In order to get there, I had to start with the basics. I had to learn how to love myself, which was no easy feat. My heart was so broken, and my spirit so wounded, that even the concept of self-love seemed foreign and out of reach.

That's when I realised that I had to start by doing the work. I had to heal myself from the inside out, and that meant addressing the trauma and pain that had been holding me back for so long. It meant doing the hard work of therapy, journaling, meditation, and of taking care of myself in every way possible.

Slowly but surely, I started to feel a shift. The pain began to lessen, and my heart started to open up to the possibility of love. I began to understand that love wasn't just a feeling, but it was also a choice. It was a decision that I could make every day, to love myself, to love those around me, and to see the beauty in the world.

I get it. I understand how hard it can be to come to that place of love, especially when you're coming from a place of trauma. But it's possible, and it starts with doing the hard work of healing and self-love. It starts with making the choice to operate from a place of love and to spread that love out into the world in everything we do.

The universe is rooting for you to live your best damn life and get everything you've ever wanted. But let's get one thing straight: you gotta start with yourself. And that means being selfish - yes, you heard me right, selfish. Because let's be real, being selfish isn't a dirty word like society makes it out to be. It just means that you prioritize your own damn self before anyone else.

So, if you want to manifest your dreams and desires, you gotta start by loving yourself. That means taking care of your mind, body, and soul. It means setting boundaries and saying "no" to things that don't serve you. It means doing what makes YOU happy, not what pleases others.

Don't let anyone guilt you into thinking that being selfish is a bad thing. The universe wants you to be selfish in the best possible way, so you can create the life you deserve. So go ahead, love yourself first and watch as the universe brings all your wildest dreams to fruition.

Here are some exercises you can try to reparent yourself and develop a more positive and supportive relationship with yourself:

1. Write a letter to your inner child: Pretend you're talking to your younger self and write them a letter of love and encouragement. Acknowledge any pain they might have felt, and let them know you're here to support them.
2. Talk to yourself kindly: Replace negative self-talk with positive and supportive words. Instead of saying "I'm not good enough," say "I am worthy of love and acceptance."
3. Be kind to yourself: When you're feeling down, show yourself some compassion and kindness. Treat yourself like you would a close friend going through a tough time.
4. Identify your needs: Figure out what you need to feel happy and fulfilled, and don't be afraid to speak up for yourself. If you need some alone time or want to set a boundary, do it!
5. Do things that make you happy: Make time for things you enjoy, like reading, taking a walk, or doing yoga. Take care of yourself and put your needs first.

Reparenting can be tough, but with practice, you can learn to be more accepting of yourself and build a more positive life. Remember, you deserve love and support!

I also believe you can 're-family', which is a concept I came up with. And you can do this through your spirit guides and ancestors who are always with you. Re-familifying with spirit guides could help cultivate a sense of belonging and support in your life.

By connecting with these guides, you may be able to tap into a source of support and guidance that can help you navigate life's challenges.

While the idea of "re-familifying" with spirit guides may not be a widely recognised term or practice, it's definitely worth exploring if it resonates with you. There are many spiritual practices and traditions that involve working with spirit guides or other forms of spiritual guidance, and you might find that connecting with your guides brings a sense of comfort and support to your life.

Starting your self-love journey is not just about healing yourself, but also allows you to start working on your love and self-worth. You need to come back to yourself and connect with the universe's source energy.

MIND/BODY/SPIRIT CONNECTION

I'm all about that mind-body-spirit connection! I mean, it's just common sense, right? Our thoughts, feelings, and beliefs are all connected to our physical and spiritual health. It's all one big happy family!

And speaking of spirituality - ooh, that's where the magic happens! It's all about finding your true self, beyond the roles and identities that society puts on you. It's about connecting with your innermost thoughts, feelings, and values, and learning to trust your own inner wisdom. Because, , you know what they say - the answers are already within you.

So let's get back to basics. The mind-body-spirit connection is all about understanding that these three aspects of our being are intimately related. They're not separate entities - they all work together to create our overall sense of well-being. So let's get in touch with our spiritual side , and start living our best life!

Let's take it back in time to the Middle Ages when beliefs about the mind-body-spirit connection started to do some serious shape-shifting. That's right, things were getting wild! Then along came Rene Descartes, a 17th-century philosopher who turned everything on its head. He popularized the idea that the mind and body were two totally separate things!

And oh boy, did that theory take off like wildfire! It influenced religious theology and medicine, shaping our conventional allopathic medical model of treating parts instead of the whole person. Yup, that's right, we've been living with the aftermath of Descartes' mind-body dualism for centuries!

But you know what they say - hindsight is 20/20! Now we know that treating the whole person is where it's at. So let's take a moment to thank Descartes for the history lesson, and then move on to bigger and better things. We're all about the mind-body-spirit connection!

Here's the deal: Your belief system is probably already filled with bits and pieces of this whole mind-body-spirit thing. It ain't rocket science! These days, you can mix and match to your heart's content. Do you want some traditional medicine with a side of complementary therapy? Go for it. Toss in some yoga and meditation, sprinkle on some religious practice, and voila! You're on your way to zen town.

You don't gotta go all-in with just one thing. Nah, a day of yoga complements your therapy sessions just as well as your morning run, healthy diet, or even your regular visits to the nail salon. So go ahead and mix it up.

The mind-body-spirit connection is all about that holistic healing, baby. You know, the kind that takes care of your physical, mental, AND spiritual well-being all at once. We're talking about a whole lotta goodness, from your thoughts and emotions to your beliefs and beyond.

And let me tell you, there's scientific evidence backing this stuff up! Practices like meditation, yoga, and mindfulness have been shown to do wonders for your mental and physical health.

In fact, some healthcare professionals are finally catching on to this whole mind-body-spirit connection thing. They know that treating patients means considering all aspects of their health, not just the physical stuff. When you address the whole shebang, you get better outcomes and improved quality of life.

When you come back to yourself, you are able to let go of external influences and societal pressures that may have been holding you back. You can embrace your authentic self and live a life that is true to your values and beliefs.

Coming back to yourself through spirituality is like giving your soul a big ol' hug. By connecting with your inner wisdom and purpose, you'll feel centred and grounded in your life. And for those who are religious, getting back to God is like finding the ultimate BFF who's always there to guide you through life's ups and downs.

I mean, let's be real, who wouldn't want to tap into a source of infinite knowledge and guidance? It's like having a spiritual Google on speed dial. By connecting with a higher power, you can gain a deeper sense of understanding about who you are and your place in the world.

Plus, prayer, meditation, and other spiritual practices can give you some serious self-reflection and introspection time. It's like having your own personal therapist, but with more candles and incense. By getting in touch with your thoughts and feelings, you can develop a stronger sense of self-awareness and become the boss of your own life.

Your internal universe is a whole other galaxy. It's like this crazy, personal world inside your mind that's shaped by everything you've ever experienced. Your thoughts, feelings, and beliefs are all part of this universe, and they reflect who you are as a person. It's like your own little world in there, just waiting to be explored.

Exploring your internal universe is where it's at! You can learn so much about yourself, your motivations, your values, and your desires. It's like taking a deep dive into the ocean of your own mind, and discovering all the hidden treasures within.

The best part? By exploring your internal universe, you can

tap into your own inner wisdom and intuition. You'll gain a clearer understanding of what you truly want, and what's really important to you. It's like having your own personal guru inside your mind, giving you all the advice and guidance you need!

And that's not all. By exploring your internal world, you'll also develop greater emotional intelligence and resilience. You'll learn how to manage your emotions in a healthy way, and find a sense of inner peace and well-being. It's like you're becoming your own emotional superhero!

So let's get ready to blast off into your own internal universe. There's a whole galaxy of self-discovery and personal growth waiting for you!

Here are 5 ways to get to know your inner world:

1. Take some "me time" and get cozy with your thoughts. Treat your inner world like a VIP guest and spend some quality time getting to know what's really going on inside your head. It's like a date with yourself, but without awkward small talk.
2. Write it out, baby! Get a pen and paper and let your thoughts flow like a river. You'll be amazed at what you can learn about yourself once you put those thoughts down on paper. It's like free therapy, but without the judgmental stares.
3. Take up meditation and get in touch with your inner zen master. By focusing on your breath and clearing your mind, you can tap into your inner wisdom and find that elusive inner peace. It's like a mental spa day, but without the expensive bill.
4. Connect with your emotions and start to feel your feels. We often try to push our emotions aside, but by acknowledging and experiencing them, we can gain a deeper understanding of ourselves. It's like a rollercoaster ride, but without nausea.

5. Talk it out with a trusted friend or therapist. Sometimes we need a little outside perspective to help us see things more clearly. By discussing our inner world with someone else, we can gain new insights and learn more about ourselves. It's like a gossip session, but without the drama.

USING YOUR POWER:

There are so many ways to tap into your powers and that's what a lot of the spiritual journey is about. You may hear a lot of people talk about being psychic or being a medium friend's dance and I truly believe that everyone has these abilities.

Being a medium and being a psychic are two different things, but there can be some overlap between the two.

A medium is someone who can communicate with spirits or the deceased. They may receive messages from loved ones who have passed away or have the ability to connect with spirits in other ways. Mediums can act as a bridge between the living and the dead and can bring comfort and closure to those who are grieving.

A psychic, on the other hand, is someone who can tap into their intuition and receive information about people, situations, or events that are not readily available through the five senses. Psychics can use various tools and techniques to access this information, such as tarot cards, astrology, or clairvoyance.

While some psychics may also have mediumistic abilities, not all mediums are necessarily psychic. Mediumship is a more specialised gift that involves communicating with spirits, while psychic abilities are broader and can encompass a range of intuitive gifts.

However, it's also possible to be both medium and a psychic. For example, a psychic medium may be able to communicate with spirits while also receiving intuitive information about the living. It's important to note that everyone's abilities are unique, and not all psychics or mediums will have the same gifts or levels of proficiency.

Let's talk all about clairvoyance, clairaudience, and all the other clairs that exist in this world. Now, some folks might think that only psychics and witches have these gifts, but let me tell you , we all have a little bit of clairvoyance in us.

Let's start with clairvoyance, which is the ability to see things beyond the physical realm. It's all about that third eye . Some folks might see visions or flashes of images, while others might just have a strong intuition or gut feeling about things. And let me tell you , that third eye can be a powerful tool for navigating this crazy world we live in.

Then we have clairaudience, which is the ability to hear things beyond the physical realm. Now, some folks might hear actual voices or sounds, while others might just get a strong sense of what someone is trying to communicate. And , if you ever hear a voice that's telling you to do something crazy, maybe give that one a second thought.

But wait, there's more! We've also got clairsentience (the ability to sense things beyond the physical realm), claircognizance (the ability to know things beyond the physical realm), and even clairgustance (the ability to taste things beyond the physical realm). Now, some folks might have one or two of these gifts, while others might have a little bit of all of them.

Now, don't go thinking that just because you don't have these gifts you're missing out on something. We all have our own unique abilities and strengths. And let me tell you , sometimes those gifts might not show up until we're a little older and wiser. So don't be afraid to explore your own intuition and see what kind of magic you can tap into.

Developing your clairvoyant and clairaudient gifts is like opening up a whole new world of intuition and perception.

You start to see things you never thought were possible and hear things you never thought you'd hear. It's like having your very own superpowers.

Now, some people are born with these gifts, while others develop them over time. It's not about being better than anyone else, it's about tapping into your own inner knowing and trusting it. It's like having a direct line to the universe, and who wouldn't want that?

If you're interested in developing your clairvoyant and clairaudient gifts, there are plenty of courses and practitioners out there who can help. Don't be afraid to reach out and ask for guidance. It's worth investing in yourself and unlocking your full potential.

But remember, just because you have these gifts doesn't mean you're exempt from hard work and practice. Developing your intuition takes time and effort, but the rewards are priceless. It's like anything else in life, the more you put into it, the more you'll get out of it.

So, if you're ready to tap into your clairvoyant and clairaudient abilities, go for it! Trust yourself and the universe, and get ready to unlock a whole new level of perception and intuition. You got this, babe!

FINDING FRIENDS:

Listen up folks, if you're going through a spiritual awakening, be prepared for some changes in your relationships and friendships. Let me tell you, the universe doesn't mess around when it comes to personal growth. And let's be real, your friends and partners may not be ready for the new and improved version of you.

First off, when you start diving deep into your spiritual journey, you may find that certain people just don't vibe with you anymore. They may not understand your new interests and perspectives, and that's okay. It's not about them not being good enough for you, it's about you outgrowing them. It's time to let go of those relationships that no longer serve you.

Another thing to expect is that some people may be threatened by your newfound sense of self. They may feel like you're leaving them behind and that can cause some tension. But remember, you can't control how others react to your growth. Just focus on staying true to yourself and let the chips fall where they may.

And let's not forget about the relationships that will deepen and strengthen during this time. You may find yourself drawn to people who are also on a spiritual journey, and those connections can be incredibly fulfilling. Don't be afraid to put yourself out there and make new friends, the universe has a way of bringing the right people into your life.

In the end, it's important to remember that change is natural and necessary for growth. And while it can be tough to let go of relationships that no longer serve you, trust that the universe will bring new and exciting connections into your life. So embrace the journey, and don't be afraid to let go of what's holding you back. The universe has got your back, babe.

When you're going through a spiritual awakening, things can get a little wild. Suddenly, you're seeing the world in a whole new light and your beliefs and priorities are shifting. This can be an exciting and empowering time, but it can also cause some major rifts in your relationships and friendships.

Why, you ask? Well, it's simple. When you're going through a spiritual awakening, you're starting to see things from a different perspective. You're becoming more in tune with your inner self and you're starting to see the world in a whole new way. This can be a beautiful thing, but it can also mean that you're no longer on the same page as the people around you.

Your friends and loved ones may not understand or agree with your new spiritual beliefs, and that can create tension and distance. They may feel like you're changing and they don't know how to relate to you anymore. They may even feel like you're leaving them behind. But here's the thing, your spiritual journey is not about anyone else but you.

Your vibration changes and you start to see things differently. And let's face it, some people just can't handle change. They want you to stay the same, but you're not that person anymore. So, it's natural for some relationships to fall apart. It's not your job to hold onto people who don't serve your growth and evolution. You're a rising star, and some folks just can't keep up with the new you. So, let them go with love and grace, and trust that the right relationships will align with your new vibration. Namaste!

It's important to remember that just because someone doesn't share your beliefs, it doesn't mean they're not important to you. It's important to communicate with your loved ones and let them know that your spiritual journey doesn't change how you feel about them. And if they don't understand or accept your spiritual journey, that's okay too. It doesn't mean you have to end your relationship, but you do have to accept that it may change.

So, what can you do about it? The best thing you can do is be open and honest with your loved ones. Let them know what you're going through and how it's affecting you. Encourage them to ask you questions and to share their feelings with you. And most importantly, don't let your spiritual journey change who you are as a person. You're still the same amazing person you always were, you just have a new perspective on life. And that's something to be proud of.

As you start to shed your old attachments - friends, hobbies, desires - you might feel a little bit like a snake trying to shed its skin. It's a wild ride, and it can last for years. Just ask me, I was a hot mess for at least 2 years and still counting.

Letting go is just part of life's process. Everything will eventually be set free, and your spiritual journey will be no exception. It doesn't matter what it is, everything must go.

The good, the bad, the beautiful, the ugly, the enlightened, and the unenlightened. This too shall pass.

Now, if you're worried about losing friends, take a moment to assess the situation. Are these friends aligned with your life's purpose? Do they support you on your path? Do they bring positivity or negativity to your life?

It can be tough to say goodbye to old friends, especially when they've been in your life for years. But here's the thing - life is all about flow. You'll have tons of friends one moment and feel like a lone wolf the next. It's just how the cookie crumbles.

The key to surviving this stage is to just go with the flow and not resist. Trust me, the more you fight, the more the universe will push back. This is all about surrendering and letting go.

The faster you surrender, the less you'll suffer. It's funny how that works, isn't it?

So, if you're feeling the pain of losing friends, embrace it. Don't fight it, dive into it. Meditate on it, feel it to the fullest. By becoming fully aware of what's going on in the moment, you'll be able to release that pain and move forward on your journey.

Just remember, the universe has got your back, and everything happens for a reason. So hold on tight, and let the journey unfold.

But let's not forget, the big spiritual awakening often happens when we're riding solo.

Of course, everyone's journey is unique. But a spiritual awakening is like a wild adventure, and it's best experienced in our own company.

And once we discover the magic of solitude and how it can turbocharge our spiritual growth and personal evolution, we might start being a little pickier about who we let into our sacred alone time.

As you continue on your journey, you may start to become more attuned to the energy of those around you. This newfound sensitivity can make you feel more protective of your own energy, as you become more aware of the impact that others have on your well-being.

Think of it like this: your energy is like a precious resource, and you want to make sure that it's being used in a positive way. When you're surrounded by negative or draining energy, it can take a toll on your physical, emotional, and spiritual state. That's why it's important to surround yourself with people who uplift and support you.

By becoming more mindful of your energy and the energy

of those around you, you can create boundaries that help you maintain your peace and balance. This doesn't mean that you should avoid people who challenge you or make you feel uncomfortable, but it does mean that you should be mindful of who you let into your inner circle and how much energy you're investing in these relationships.

Meeting new spiritual friends can be a wonderful way to connect with like-minded individuals and expand your spiritual journey. Here are some ways to meet new spiritual friends:

1. Attend spiritual events: Look for spiritual workshops, retreats, or conferences in your area and attend them. You'll have the opportunity to connect with others who share your interests and values. There are so many websites for this, including Eventbrite, meetup.com and many more where you can find things around your area and online.

2. Join a spiritual group: Search for spiritual groups in your community, such as meditation groups, spiritual discussion groups, or yoga classes. This is a great way to meet others who are on a similar path.

3. Volunteer for a spiritual organisation: Volunteering for a spiritual organisation is a great way to give back and meet new people.

4. Online communities: There are many online communities dedicated to spirituality and personal growth. There's also an app that I created for this very reason, which is called Woo Woo. You can also book readers in astrologers and healers there. Message new friends and ask questions in the forms. We created it with you in mind.Join these communities and engage in discussions, attend virtual events, and connect with others who share your interests.

5. Seek out a spiritual mentor: Finding a spiritual

mentor can be a great way to deepen your spiritual practice and make new connections.

And transparently I started a business around this whole idea because finding friends is super hard! Not to mention finding the right guides and healers, to help you on your journey as well. It's called woo and it's currently on the App Store and coming to Android soon. You can find spiritual friends and talk to them, message them in the forums, as well as book tarot readers, astrologers and healers. More on www.joinwoowoo.com.

CHAPTER 7: MINDSET & MANIFESTING

For a long time, I really didn't understand the concept of manifesting and it really sounded like bullshit, to be honest.. I also thought that you couldn't just make a wish and have it happen, but that's not really what manifests, to be honest.

It's all about using your thoughts and emotions to attract positive experiences and things into your life. The way it works is by focusing your mind on what you want and letting the universe do the rest.

There are some universal laws that come into play, like the Law of Attraction and the Law of Vibration, which basically say that you attract what you think about and that everything in the universe is connected by energy. So if you think positive thoughts and feel good about what you want, you'll attract more of that into your life.

To manifest your desires, you need to be clear about what you want, believe that it's possible, and take action towards your goals. It's not just about sitting around and waiting for things to happen magically, but rather about aligning your thoughts, emotions, and actions with your desired outcome. Trust in the universe to help you out and be patient as things unfold. With a little practice, you can start manifesting the life of your dreams!

Manifesting is not just about setting your intentions and hoping for the best - it's also about taking action towards your goals. Your intuition can be a powerful guide in this process, leading you towards the next steps that will bring you closer to making your dreams a reality.

When you follow your intuition, you're tapping into your inner wisdom and guidance system. This can help you to make decisions and take actions that are aligned with your true desires and purpose. Your intuition might nudge you towards certain opportunities or people that can help you on your path, or it might give you a sense of clarity and direction when you're feeling unsure.

So, while manifesting is about using your thoughts and emotions to attract positive experiences and things into your life, it's also about taking inspired action towards your goals. By listening to your intuition and following its guidance, you can take steps that feel aligned with your purpose and move towards the life you want to create. Remember, the universe is always conspiring in your favour, but you have to do your part too!

I've noticed that when I'm still operating from a place of trauma, it's really hard for me to manifest the things that I want. I've struggled with this for a long time, and it can be really frustrating to feel like my desires are always out of reach.

However, I've also noticed that as I work on my healing and clear out the blockages in my energy field, manifesting becomes much easier. When I take the time to prioritize my self-care and do the work to heal my heart, I'm able to raise my vibration and become more in tune with the universe. This makes it easier to attract the things I want into my life, and I feel more aligned with my desires.

Of course, healing is not a linear process, and there are times when old traumas or patterns resurface. But I've learned that by staying committed to my healing and continuing to do the work, I can stay in alignment with my desires and keep manifesting the things I want in my life.
Overall, I've come to realise that my mindset and energy play a big role in my ability to manifest.

LET'S TALK ABOUT THE BRAIN AND REALITY:

Your brain is like a powerful computer that can be programmed to work for you or against you. If you're constantly feeding it negative thoughts and limiting beliefs, that's exactly what it's going to give you in return. But if you take the time to reprogram your mind with positive thoughts and beliefs, it will work tirelessly to manifest those things into your reality.

Your thoughts and beliefs shape your perception of reality, which in turn shapes your experiences and outcomes. If you believe that life is full of opportunities, you may find yourself noticing and pursuing more opportunities, leading to a more fulfilling and successful life. On the other hand, if you believe that life is difficult and unfair, you may experience more setbacks and challenges, leading to a less fulfilling and potentially unhappy life.

This concept is rooted in the idea of the law of attraction, which suggests that you attract into your life the things that you focus on, whether positive or negative. The law of attraction suggests that the universe responds to your thoughts and beliefs by bringing you experiences that align with them. Therefore, by intentionally focusing your thoughts and beliefs on what you want to create in your life, you can shape your reality and manifest your desired outcomes.

So if you're serious about manifesting the life you desire, you need to start paying attention to your thoughts and beliefs. Stop letting your mind run wild with negative self-talk and start taking control of it. Trust me, when you start aligning your mind with the universal laws, the results will be nothing short of amazing.

When folks first stumble upon the Law of Attraction, they start realising just how much negative thinking they're actually doing. And of course, like a bolt of lightning, they freak out because they think those bad vibes are going to instantly materialise into their reality. But listen up - negative thoughts happen to the best of us. Even the most positive folks out there have a crummy thought every now and then. It's not even really your thought to begin with, it's just something that's floating around in the shared consciousness of humanity. So don't go wasting your time trying to analyse every single thought that pops into your head. What matters is what you choose to focus on. That's what actually manifests.

Limiting beliefs are thoughts or ideas that hold us back and prevent us from achieving our goals and living the life we truly desire. These beliefs can be formed in a variety of ways, but they all stem from past experiences and the way we interpret them.

One of the main ways limiting beliefs are created is through childhood experiences. As children, we are highly impressionable and tend to believe everything we are told. If we are repeatedly told that we are not good enough, smart enough, or capable of achieving certain things, we may internalize those beliefs and carry them with us into adulthood. These negative messages can also come from parents, teachers, peers or even through the media, shaping our beliefs about ourselves and the world around us.

Another way limiting beliefs are created is through past failures and setbacks. If we experience a disappointment or setback, it's natural to want to understand why it happened. However, if we interpret the event in a negative way and blame ourselves, it can lead to the formation of limiting beliefs. For example, if someone has been rejected in a job interview and starts to believe that they are not qualified enough, this belief can limit their future job opportunities.

Lastly, limiting beliefs can also be created through societal or cultural conditioning. We live in a society that often promotes certain standards and ideals, and if we don't fit into those norms, it can lead us to believe that something is wrong with us. For example, if someone is not conventionally attractive, they may believe that they are not attractive enough. This belief can limit their dating life and self-esteem. These beliefs hold us back and prevent us from reaching our goals. Recognizing and addressing them is an important step towards manifesting the life we truly desire.

There are several ways to overcome limiting beliefs and replace them with empowering ones. Here are a few methods:

1. recognise and challenge them: The first step in overcoming limiting beliefs is recognizing that they exist. Once you're aware of them, you can start to challenge them by questioning the evidence for and against them. Is there any evidence that supports the belief, or is it just a thought you've been telling yourself?

2. Reframe your thoughts: Once you've identified a limiting belief, try reframing it into a more positive and empowering thought. For example, instead of thinking "I'm not good enough," try saying "I am capable and have the skills to achieve my goals."

3. Practice self-compassion: Limiting beliefs often stem from negative self-talk and self-criticism.

Practicing self-compassion can help to counteract these negative thoughts and beliefs. Self-compassion involves treating yourself with the same kindness, concern, and understanding you would offer to a good friend.

4. Take action: Taking action towards your goals is a powerful way to overcome limiting beliefs. By taking small steps towards your goal, you can begin to see that you are capable and start to build momentum.

5. Seek professional help: If you find it difficult to overcome limiting beliefs on your own, seeking professional help can be beneficial. A therapist or coach can help you to understand the origin of your limiting beliefs, develop strategies to overcome them, and support you in your journey towards achieving your goals.

AVOID THE MEDIA AS MUCH AS POSSIBLE:

Can we talk about the media for a sec? They're all up in our faces, trying to scare the pants off us with their constant barrage of negative, fear-mongering content. Like seriously, it's like they're addicted to murder, death, and betrayal. It's no wonder our minds are fixated on all the bad stuff that's happening, instead of focusing on the good.

But hey, don't get me wrong, there are some glimmers of hope out there. And it's high time we start shining a light on those inspirational stories and positive messages. 'Cause , once that momentum starts rolling, it's unstoppable. Like a freakin' domino effect, those good vibes are gonna keep on comin'.

So don't let the media bring you down. Keep your eyes peeled for those uplifting stories and surround yourself with positive people and messages. 'Cause let's face it, life's too short to be fixated on all the doom and gloom. Let's focus on the good stuff and spread that positivity like wildfire.

Now, I'm not gonna coat it - the news can be a real downer. It's filled with all sorts of negativity, from murders to political scandals to natural disasters. But, if you're up for the challenge, watching the news can actually help you cultivate a better mindset.

How, you ask? Well, for starters, it can give you a sense of perspective. It's easy to get caught up in our own little bubble and forget that there's a whole world out there. But watching the news can remind us of the challenges and struggles that others are facing, and help us to appreciate our own blessings.

Secondly, it can inspire you to take action. When you see stories of people making a difference or communities coming together, it can motivate you to get involved and make a positive impact.

But here's the catch - you gotta be discerning. Don't just take everything the news says at face value. Take the time to fact-check and seek out different perspectives. And, most importantly, don't let it consume you. Don't spend hours upon hours glued to the screen, or else you'll just end up feeling overwhelmed and helpless.

So, if you're up for the challenge, go ahead and watch the news. Just remember to keep a healthy perspective and don't let it bring you down. 'Cause let's face it, life's too short to be living in a constant state of despair.

GO STRAIGHT TO THE ROOT:

Another powerful way to overcome your limiting beliefs is to go straight to the unconscious. And hypnotherapy is a great way to do that. Hypnotherapy is a powerful tool for overcoming limiting beliefs and reprogramming the subconscious mind. When you are in a state of hypnosis, your mind is more open to suggestion and change, making it an ideal state for addressing limiting beliefs and reprogramming the mind with positive thoughts and beliefs.

During hypnotherapy, a trained practitioner will guide you into a state of deep relaxation, where you are more open to suggestions. They will then work with you to uncover and address any limiting beliefs that may be holding you back. They will also provide you with positive affirmations and suggestions that can help to reprogram your subconscious mind with more empowering thoughts and beliefs.

One of the key benefits of hypnotherapy is that it allows you to bypass the critical mind and directly access the subconscious mind. The subconscious mind is responsible for shaping our behaviour, habits and beliefs, and it's often the source of limiting beliefs. By working directly with the subconscious mind, hypnotherapy can help to quickly and effectively overcome limiting beliefs and change the way you think and behave.

Additionally, hypnotherapy can help to reduce anxiety and

stress, which can be a major obstacle in overcoming limiting beliefs. It's common for people to be in a state of anxiety and stress when they are trying to change their limiting beliefs, hypnotherapy can help to reduce these feelings and create a sense of calm and relaxation, making it easier to reprogram your mind with positive thoughts and beliefs.

In summary, hypnotherapy is a powerful tool for overcoming limiting beliefs by working directly with the subconscious mind, providing positive affirmations and suggestions, reducing anxiety and stress and creating a sense of calm and relaxation, making it easier to reprogram the mind with positive thoughts and beliefs. It is important to work with a trained practitioner who understands how to use hypnotherapy for this purpose.

Limiting beliefs only have any power, when they're operating in the unconscious. Once you bring them into your consciousness and you can see them for what they are, this is when you can start to work on them. One of the easiest ways to do this is by journaling about this. And take it from the person that really didn't like journaling, this is one of the most powerful things that I did. Some of the questions you can answer in your journal is:

1. "What are the negative thoughts and beliefs that hold me back from achieving my goals?"
2. "What experiences in my past have contributed to my limiting beliefs?"
3. "In what areas of my life do I have the most difficulty with limiting beliefs?"
4. "What are some examples of limiting beliefs that I have about myself?"
5. "What are some examples of limiting beliefs that I have about others?"
6. "How do my limiting beliefs affect my relationships and interactions with others?"

7. "What would my life look like without my limiting beliefs?"
8. "What are some positive affirmations that I can use to counter my limiting beliefs?"
9. "What actions can I take today to overcome my limiting beliefs?"
10. "What support do I need in order to overcome my limiting beliefs?"

These prompts are designed to encourage reflection on limiting beliefs, how they were formed and how they are affecting your life, as well as potential ways to overcome them. It's important to remember that uncovering and dealing with limiting beliefs is a process and it takes time and effort to change the way you think.

FEEL INTO IT

Feelings are the way that we communicate vibrationally with the universe and therefore, they are crucial to the manifestation process. Every feeling that we experience carries a certain frequency or vibration, whether it is a high vibrational emotion such as love, joy, or gratitude, or a low vibrational emotion such as fear, anger, or sadness.

According to the Law of Attraction, like attracts like. So, if we are experiencing and feeling positive emotions, we are sending out a high frequency that will attract positive experiences, people, and things into our lives. On the other hand, if we are experiencing and feeling negative emotions, we are sending out a low frequency that will attract negative experiences, people, and things into our lives.

Therefore, if we want to manifest our desires and attract what we want into our lives, it is essential to focus on feeling the feelings of what we would feel if we had the manifestation. This can be done through various practices, such as gratitude journaling, visualization, affirmations, and meditation.

By holding the frequency of what we want to manifest through our feelings, we are effectively aligning ourselves with that which we desire, and signalling to the universe that we are ready to receive it. The universe will then respond by bringing us experiences, people, and things that match the frequency of our emotions and help us to manifest our desires into reality.

An example? When people think about money, they usually associate it with freedom. They believe that having money will give them the freedom they desire, so they manifest it. The same goes for finding a partner - they want to feel loved, so they manifest a partner to bring that love into their life. On the flip side, our fears are also rooted in our feelings. When we fear failure or rejection, we're really just trying to avoid feeling a certain way. We want to feel good, but we're afraid of feeling bad if things don't work out. And that's where we get stuck. We end up avoiding our feelings and doing nothing. But here's the thing - feelings are important in manifestation because they're how we communicate with the universe. When we feel good, we attract good things, and vice versa. But a lot of folks don't realise that resisting bad feelings only makes them stronger. You gotta let 'em flow through you and move on. And don't forget, feelings drive our behaviour. They come from our thoughts, which create our actions and ultimately manifest into our reality. So if you want to change your life, you gotta start with your thoughts and feelings. No need for a fancy class, just sit on your couch and process those emotions, baby.

It's important to acknowledge that feeling good all the time is not a realistic expectation for anyone. We all go through challenges, hardships, and difficult emotions from time to time. It's not healthy or helpful to ignore or suppress these emotions in the name of maintaining a positive attitude.

Ignoring negative emotions and pretending to feel positive all the time is what is known as "spiritual bypassing." It's important to address and work through our negative emotions and not just try to push them aside. Healing from trauma and difficult emotions is a process that takes time, and it's essential to allow ourselves to feel and process our emotions fully.

That being said, it's important to understand that the way we feel most of the time has a significant impact on the things we attract into our lives. If we are constantly feeling negative emotions, we are more likely to attract negative experiences and outcomes. Conversely, if we are mostly feeling positive emotions, we are more likely to attract positive experiences and outcomes.

The key is not to force ourselves to feel positive all the time, but rather to cultivate a general sense of positivity and optimism by focusing on things that make us feel good and engaging in self-care practices that promote positive emotions. Additionally, it's important to give ourselves grace and compassion when we are going through difficult times and not beat ourselves up for not feeling positive all the time. It's about finding a balance between acknowledging and processing our negative emotions and working towards cultivating positive emotions and a positive outlook overall.

TRAUMA AND MANIFESTING:

Earlier in this book, we talked about the dark night of the soul, and it's true that a significant part of the spiritual journey involves healing your trauma so that you can operate from a clear and high-vibrational space. This is because our past experiences and emotions can create energetic blocks and distortions that cloud our ability to manifest our desires.

When we're operating from a low frequency due to trauma, it can be challenging to manifest the life we want. Our energy is scattered and unfocused, making it difficult to channel our intention and attract what we truly desire. It's like trying to drive a car with a dirty windshield - you can't see where you're going clearly, and you're more likely to crash or take a wrong turn.

That's why doing the healing work is so crucial to the manifestation process. By addressing our trauma and releasing the negative energy that's been holding us back, we can clear the way for our intentions to manifest with greater ease and speed.

In the past six to twelve months, I've found it significantly easier to manifest my desires than ever before. And I think the reason for this is that I've done some serious work on myself through various forms of healing.

I've explored kinesiology, shamanic healing, Reiki healing, and therapy, all of which have helped me to step more fully into who I am and remember my true self. Through this healing work, I've been able to let go of the wounded victim mentality that was holding me back and release the pain that had been stored in my body.

As a result of this healing, my vibration has naturally become higher and happier. I'm operating from a place of greater clarity, positivity, and self-love, which makes it easier for me to focus on my desires and manifest them into reality.

It's amazing how much our inner state affects our ability to manifest. When we're carrying around negative energy and unresolved emotions, it can create energetic blocks that prevent us from attracting what we truly desire. But when we do the work to heal ourselves, we can remove those blocks and allow our energy to flow freely.

Of course, healing work isn't always easy. It can be challenging and require a lot of effort and dedication. But the rewards are immeasurable. When we take the time to heal ourselves, we not only improve our ability to manifest, but we also create a life that feels more aligned with our true purpose and potential.

So if you're struggling to manifest your desires, consider doing some inner work to heal yourself. Whether it's through therapy, energy healing, or any other modality, taking the time to care for yourself and release any negative energy can make all the difference in your ability to create the life you truly desire.

Of course, this isn't always an easy or straightforward process. Healing can be messy, painful, and require a lot of time and effort. But it's worth it, honey. Because when we do the work to heal our trauma and raise our vibration, we not only manifest our desires more easily, but we also create a life that's more aligned with our highest purpose and potential.

When we carry unresolved trauma, it can create energetic blocks and distortions in our energy field, which can lower our vibration and make it harder to manifest our desires. It's like carrying a heavy backpack that weighs us down and makes it harder to move forward.

By doing the work to heal our trauma, we can release these blocks and distortions and raise our vibration to a higher frequency. This makes it easier to manifest our desires and attract positive experiences into our lives.

So don't be afraid to dive deep and do the healing work, babe. It may be hard, but it's the key to unlocking your true power and potential as a manifestor.

THE UNIVERSAL LAWS

Well, well, well, it seems like everyone and their mother is talking about the "Law of Attraction" these days, all thanks to that little movie called "The Secret." But let me tell you, , the Law of Attraction is just the tip of the iceberg when it comes to understanding universal laws. Sure, it's an important one, but have you ever heard of the Law of Vibration? The Law of Cause and Effect? The Law of Compensation? I didn't think so. People these days want the secret to success to be as simple as just thinking positive thoughts, but the truth is, it takes more than that. It takes understanding and utilizing all 12 universal laws to truly manifest the life you desire. So go ahead and keep thinking happy thoughts, but don't forget to educate yourself on the other 11 laws too

The universe is a mysterious place and it follows certain laws that govern it. And these laws are non-negotiable, so better pay attention!

The Law of Oneness - We are all connected and everything is interconnected.

The Law of Oneness is a basic principle that states that we are all interconnected and everything is interconnected. It means that everything in the universe is part of a single, unified whole, and that everything is connected to everything else. It's like a cosmic web of energy and we are all part of it.

Think about it, when you're feeling good, you're sending out positive vibes and it affects everyone around you. And when you're feeling down, it affects everyone around you too. We're all in this together, babe.

And this law applies to everything, from the tiniest microbe to the biggest galaxy. We're all connected and everything is connected. It's a beautiful thing, really.

So, next time you're feeling isolated and alone, remember that you're not. We're all in this together and we're all connected. Now go out there and spread love, and it'll come back to you tenfold.

1. **The Law of Vibration - Everything in the universe is energy and it vibrates at a certain frequency.** The Law of Vibration states that everything in the universe is energy and it vibrates at a certain frequency. Everything, from the chair you're sitting on to the thoughts in your head, is vibrating energy.

And get this, you have the power to control the frequency at which you vibrate. When you're feeling good, your energy vibrates at a higher frequency, and when you're feeling bad, your energy vibrates at a lower frequency. It's like a radio station, you can tune into different frequencies depending on how you're feeling.

So, if you want to attract good things into your life, you need to raise your vibration. How do you do that? By being grateful, by practicing positivity and by surrounding yourself with good vibes.

And on the other hand, if you're constantly focusing on negative thoughts and energy, you'll attract more of the same. It's that simple.

So, you better start paying attention to the frequency at which you're vibrating and make sure it's a high one. Trust me, it'll make all the difference in the world.

The Law of Action - Nothing can manifest without taking action.

The Law of Action is like the ultimate wake-up call. It states that nothing can manifest without taking action. Yup, you heard that right, you can't just sit around and wait for things to happen, you gotta make them happen.

It's like a recipe, you can have all the ingredients in the world, but if you don't take action and bake the cake, it ain't gonna happen.

So, if you want to manifest your desires and bring positive things into your life, you gotta take action. And not just any action, but purposeful, intentional action. It's time to stop making excuses and start making things happen.

And don't forget, taking action doesn't mean just working hard, it also means taking care of your mind, body, and spirit. It's about being in alignment with what you truly want and taking steps towards that.

So, don't just sit there, take action and make things happen. Trust me, you won't regret it.

The Law of Correspondence - Your inner world corresponds to your outer world.

The Law of Correspondence is like a mirror image of your thoughts and emotions. It states that your inner world corresponds to your outer world. Meaning, what's happening in your mind is reflected in your reality.

It's like a boomerang, what you put out there comes back to you. So, if you're constantly thinking negative thoughts, you'll attract negative experiences into your life. But, if you're thinking positive thoughts, you'll attract positive experiences.

It's time to start paying attention to the thoughts you're having, and if they're not serving you, it's time to change them.

Start being mindful of your thoughts and make sure they align with what you truly want.

And don't forget, your emotions are just as powerful as your thoughts. So, if you want to start attracting positive experiences, start feeling good. It's that simple.

So, take a look at your inner world and start aligning it with what you want in your outer world

The Law of Cause and Effect - Every action has a reaction.

The Law of Cause and Effect is like the ultimate accountability partner. It states that every action has a reaction, so you better start being mindful of the actions you're taking.

It's like a domino effect, every action you take sets off a chain of events. So, if you're constantly making negative choices, you'll attract negative experiences. But, if you're making positive choices, you'll attract positive experiences.

It's time to start taking responsibility for the actions you're taking and the experiences you're attracting. And remember, it's not just about the big choices, it's also about the small ones. Every choice you make, no matter how insignificant it may seem, has an effect on your life.

So, start being mindful of the choices you're making and make sure they align with what you truly want. It's time to start taking control of your life, and the Law of Cause and Effect is the perfect tool to do it.

And remember, the power is in your hands, you can choose to make it a positive or negative experience, but you can't blame anyone else for the outcome.

The Law of Compensation - The universe will compensate you for your thoughts, feelings, and actions.

The Law of Compensation states that the universe will compensate you for your thoughts, feelings, and actions. It means that what you put out there, you'll get back.

It's like a cosmic bank account, every time you deposit positive thoughts, feelings, and actions, you'll earn interest in the form of positive experiences. But, if you're constantly depositing negative thoughts, feelings, and actions, you'll earn interest in the form of negative experiences.

So, if you want to start attracting positive experiences into your life, start depositing positive thoughts, feelings, and actions. Cultivate a positive attitude, practice gratitude, and take purposeful action towards what you truly want.

And remember, the universe is always watching, and it'll compensate you accordingly. So, start investing in yourself and watch how it pays off.

The Law of Attraction - Like attracts like.

The Law of Attraction is like a magnet, it states that like attracts like. So, if you're constantly putting out positive vibes, you'll attract positive experiences into your life. But, if you're putting out negative vibes, you'll attract negative experiences.

It's time to start paying attention to the energy you're putting out there and make sure it aligns with what you truly want. And don't be fooled, it's not just about thinking positive thoughts, it's also about feeling positive emotions. Your thoughts and emotions are energy, and they have a frequency.

So, start cultivating a positive attitude, practice gratitude, and surround yourself with good vibes. It's time to start attracting the life you truly want.

And remember, it's not just about attracting material things, it's also about attracting the right people, experiences and opportunities into your life.

So, start putting out positive energy, and watch how it starts attracting positive experiences into your life.

The Law of Perpetual Transmutation of Energy - Energy can change form but it cannot be destroyed.

The Law of Perpetual Transmutation of Energy is like the ultimate recycling program. It states that energy can change form but it cannot be destroyed.

It means that everything in the universe is made of energy and that energy is constantly changing and transforming. And the best part is, you have the power to control the form that energy takes.

So, if you're constantly putting out negative energy, it'll come back to you in the form of negative experiences. But, if you're putting out positive energy, it'll come back to you in the form of positive experiences.

It's time to start paying attention to the energy you're putting out there and make sure it aligns with what you truly want. And remember, energy is not just physical, it's also mental and emotional.

Start cultivating a positive attitude, practice gratitude, and surround yourself with good vibes. It's time to start attracting the life you truly want.

And remember, the energy you put out there never disappears, it's always present, it only changes forms. So choose wisely the energy you want to put out there

The Law of Relativity - Everything is relative to something else.

The Law of Relativity is like the ultimate perspective check. It states that everything is relative to something else.

It means that everything in the universe is relative to something else and that there's no such thing as absolute truth. It's all about perspective.

It's time to start seeing things from different angles and understanding that there's no one right way to see things. It's about understanding that your reality is subjective and that other people have different realities.

It's time to start being open-minded and understanding that the world is a big place and there are many ways to see things. And remember, understanding the law of relativity will help you to be more understanding and compassionate towards others.

So, start seeing things from different angles and understand that your reality is just one of many. It's time to start being open-minded and understanding that the world is a big place and there are many ways to see things. Trust me, it'll make all the difference.

The Law of Polarity - Everything has an opposite.

The Law of Polarity is like the ultimate yin and yang. It states that everything has an opposite. It means that everything in the universe has an opposite and that there's no such thing as pure good or pure bad.

It's time to start understanding that everything is relative and that everything has a balance. And remember, it's not just about good and bad, it's also about light and dark, hot and cold, and so on.

It's time to start accepting the duality of life and understanding that everything has its opposite. And remember, understanding this law will help you to be more understanding and accepting of the different aspects of life.

So, start accepting the duality of life and understand that everything has its opposite. Trust me, it'll make all the difference

The Law of Rhythm - Everything moves in a rhythm.

The Law of Rhythm is like the ultimate dance partner. It states that everything moves in a rhythm. Everything in the universe, from the smallest atom to the largest galaxy, follows a rhythm, a pattern, a flow.

It's time to start understanding that life is not static, it's fluid and ever-changing. And remember, it's not just about the good times, it's also about the bad times, the ups and downs, the ebbs and flows.

It's time to start going with the flow and understanding that everything has its own rhythm. And remember, understanding this law will help you to be more understanding and accepting of the different aspects of life.

So, start going with the flow and understand that everything has its own rhythm. Trust me, it'll make all the difference

The Law of Gender - Everything has a masculine and feminine aspect.

The Law of Gender is like the ultimate balance. It states that everything has a masculine and feminine aspect. It means that everything in the universe has a balance of masculine and feminine energy.

It's time to start understanding that there's no such thing as purely masculine or purely feminine. Everything has a balance and it's time to start embracing both aspects.

And remember, it's not just about gender, it's also about the balance of yin and yang, active and passive, giving and receiving.

It's time to start embracing both aspects of yourself and understand that balance is key. And remember, understanding this law will help you to be more understanding and accepting of the different aspects of yourself and others.

So, start embracing both aspects of yourself and understand

that balance is key.

So, remember that these laws are always at play and you can use them to your advantage.

In conclusion, understanding and working with the 12 universal laws is essential for manifesting abundance and success in all areas of life. These laws provide a powerful framework for creating the reality we desire, but they also require discipline and consistent effort to implement. It is not enough to simply know about these laws, one must take action and actively work with them to see real results. Those who are willing to put in the time and energy to align themselves with these universal principles will be rewarded with a life of abundance and fulfilment. But for those who choose to ignore these laws, the consequences can be dire. So let us remember, the power of the universe is at our fingertips, but it is up to us to seize it and make it work for us.

IT'S TIME TO LOOK AT YOUR LIFE:

So now that you know what the laws are and also how to start working on your limiting beliefs, we also need to look at where you are right now in life. You can't expect to get to where you wanna go if you don't know where you currently are. So, let's get real. Are you surrounded by people that make you feel good about yourself and support you? Is your money situation one that you feel happy with? Are you in a job or business that you like? Are you happy with what you see when you look at yourself in the mirror?

Play getting crystal clear and looking at your life as it is right now, it's indicative of what you believe about yourself, because what you believe creates your story which then creates your identity and in turn, your behaviour.

So, ask yourself this crucial question: "What do I believe to be true?"

If you're feeling frustrated, stressed out, and angry, it's time for a change. And change begins with self-awareness. So, take a good look at your life and ask yourself what you truly want and what you truly believe. Because that's the first step to creating the life you deserve.

In short, you can't expect to get to where you wanna go if you don't know where you currently are. So, take a good look at your life, relationships, business, career, health, and every other area. Get real with yourself and ask the important question, "What do I believe to be true?" Because, that's the key to creating the life you deserve.

An easy way that I did this was to simply score different areas of my life out of 10, with 10 being the best and one being the worst. This showed how I felt about them and it was really eye-opening.

Scoring every area of your life out of 10 is a great way to understand how you're doing and how you feel about your life. It can help you identify areas that you're excelling in, as well as areas that you may need to focus on to improve. Here's an explanation of how to score each area:

1. Relationships: This area includes your relationships with friends, family, and romantic partners. Consider how healthy, fulfilling, and supportive these relationships are, and give them a score out of 10.

2. Career: This area includes your job, business, or any other pursuit that you engage in to make a living. Consider how satisfied you are with your job, how much you're earning, and how much room for growth there is. Give this area a score out of 10.

3. Health: This area includes both physical and mental health. Consider how well you're taking care of your body, how much exercise you're getting, and how well you're managing your mental health. Give this area a score out of 10.

4. Finances: This area includes your income, expenses, savings, and investments. Consider how financially stable you feel and how much you're able to save. Give this area a score out of 10.

5. Personal Development: This area includes your growth, learning, and self-improvement. Consider how much you're growing, learning and developing as a person. Give this area a score out of 10.

6. Spirituality/Mindfulness: This area includes your spiritual practices, mindfulness and connection to something bigger. Consider how connected you feel to something greater and how much time you spend on self-reflection and inner-work. Give this area a score out of 10.

Once you've scored each area, you'll have a better understanding of how you're doing overall and where you might need to focus your attention. Remember that you can always work on improving in any area, and there's always room for growth and progress.

Scoring each area of your life out of 10 is a powerful way to gain insight into how you're feeling about different aspects of your life. It can help you identify areas that are going well and areas that may need improvement. If you score an area under five, it's a clear indication that you may want to make some changes in that area of your life.

Scoring an area under five indicates that you're not satisfied with that area of your life. It may be a sign that you're not happy with your relationships, your job, your health, your finances, or your personal development.

Low scores in certain areas can be a sign of imbalance in your life. For example, if you score your career a 10 but your relationships a 3, it might indicate that you're working too hard and not spending enough time with loved ones.

When you score an area under five, it's an opportunity to reflect on what changes you need to make in order to improve that area of your life. It might mean setting new goals, developing new habits, or seeking professional help.

Scoring each area of your life out of 10 and identifying low scores, is an indication that it's time to take action. It's a reminder that you have the power to change your life and create the life you want.

MANIFESTATION TECHNIQUES:

We've looked at where we are in life and we understand now the universal laws and how they work with manifestation.

It's important to remember that the universe isn't some bumbling idiot that needs you to keep reminding it of what you want. It's the creator of everything, from the stars in the sky to the flowers in your backyard. So when you're manifesting, don't think you have to keep repeating your cosmic order like some broken record. Trust me, the universe has got this.

When you make a request, the universe hears you loud and clear, and it's already working to bring it to you. You don't have to keep reminding it of what you want, because it's already on it. So, instead of focusing on constantly putting in your order, focus on being open and receptive to receiving it.

Think of it like ordering a pizza. You call up the pizza place and place your order, but do you keep calling them every five minutes to remind them of what you want? No, you trust that they heard you the first time and that your pizza is on its way. And when it arrives, you don't check the box a hundred times to make sure it's the right pizza. You trust that it is.

The same goes for the universe. When you make a request, trust that it's been heard and that it's on its way to you. Don't keep asking for it over and over again, because the universe isn't some cosmic pizza delivery guy. It's the creator of everything, and it doesn't need you to remind it of what you want. So, relax and let the universe do its thing. And when your manifestation arrives, don't question it, just enjoy it.

So with that in mind, here are some of my top ways to manifest what you want with the universe.

1. **Get clear on what you want. Like, really clear. Write it down, make a vision board, or whatever helps you get crystal clear on your desires.**

If you want to manifest your desires, you gotta get real clear on what they are. I'm talking crystal clear. Not just a general idea, but a detailed description of exactly what you want. Write it down, make a vision board, do whatever it takes to get clear on your desires. Trust me, this is the first step to making your dreams a reality.

But why is it so important to be specific about what you want? Well, for one thing, if you're not clear on what you want, how do you expect the universe to know? It's like trying to order a drink at a bar without telling the bartender what you want. You're gonna be standing there all night without a drink in hand. So, get clear on what you want and communicate it to the universe loud and clear.

And don't be shy about what you want either. You deserve to have it all, girl. Don't hold back or be afraid to ask for what you really want. You're not being selfish or greedy, you're just being clear on what you want. And when you're clear, you give the universe the opportunity to bring it to you.

If you don't know what you want, then another great way to do this is a question Ellie. Here are some of the journal prompts that I used to get super clear about what it is that I do want. PS you can also use what you don't want as a starting point.

1. "What do you want, even if it seems impossible or ridiculous?"

2. "What would your life look like if you had everything you ever wanted?"
3. "What are the top three things you would do if you had no limitations or fears?"
4. "What do you want so badly that it keeps you up at night?"
5. "What would you do if you won the lottery tomorrow? What does that say about what you truly want?"

VISUALIZATION:

Visualisation is one of my favourite techniques for manifesting my desires. It's a powerful tool that allows me to create a clear mental picture of what I want and feel as if it's already happened. By using my imagination and my senses, I can create a detailed vision of my desired outcome and feel the emotions associated with it.

One of the things I love most about visualisation is that it's so versatile. I can use it to manifest anything from a new job to a new romantic partner to a new home. Whatever it is that I want, I can use visualization to help me get there.

If you want to manifest your desires, you've got to use your imagination and feel the emotions of achieving your goal as if it's already happened. So, close those beautiful eyes of yours and picture your desire in vivid detail, using all your senses. See it, taste it, smell it, touch it, and hear it.

Let's say you're manifesting a new job, darling. Picture yourself walking into that fancy office on your first day, feeling like a boss babe. Take note of the little details, like the sound of your heels clicking on the floor, the smell of fresh coffee, and the feel of your handbag swinging by your side.

And don't forget to feel the emotions associated with achieving your desire. Get pumped up, excited, and grateful like you've already got it in the bag, babe. You've got this!

The key to making it work is to create a mental picture that's so vivid and compelling that it feels like it's already happened. So, use your imagination and let your emotions run wild, honey. You're unstoppable! Just remember, visualization is only one piece of the puzzle. Keep your thoughts and beliefs aligned with your goals, take inspired action, and watch the magic unfold.

SCRIPTING:

Scripting is a powerful manifestation technique that can help you bring your desires into reality. It involves writing down your goals and dreams as if they have already happened, in present tense. This process helps to align your thoughts and feelings with your desired outcome, making it more likely for it to manifest in your life.

Here's an explanation of how to do scripting:

1. Start by identifying your desired outcome or goal. It can be anything from a new job, a relationship, or financial abundance, to good health.
2. Once you have identified your goal, write it down in the present tense as if it has already happened. For example, "I am so happy and grateful now that I have landed my dream job" or "I am in a loving and fulfilling relationship with the perfect partner for me".
3. Be specific and detailed in your writing. Include as many sensory details as possible, such as how you feel, what you see, what you hear, and so on. The more specific and detailed you are, the more real it will feel to you.

Scripting is a powerful manifestation technique because it helps you to align your thoughts and feelings with your desired outcome. When you write your goals and dreams as if they have already happened, it sends a strong message to the universe that you are ready and open to receiving it. It also helps to increase your belief in the possibility of achieving your goal, which is crucial for manifestation to happen.

If you're not one for using pen and paper, an easy way to do this is to use your voice to type on your notes on your phone. I do this for journaling, and I've also used my voice to write a lot of this book. And that didn't turn out so bad, did it? I find that sometimes the process of using a pen, although it can be beneficial, is too slow for how fast my brain works. You can take it a step further and use it to write about different scripts for your life, or you could use it to write about your day as though the things you want to manifest have already happened, like you're writing at the end of the day. That's working with the law of assumption right there, and it's damn powerful. You can also take this to the next level and use voice notes to do the same thing each day, talking about what you're grateful for as though it's already happened, and talking about your life or situation as though you're being interviewed by someone famous on a podcast, telling the story of how all of your success happened. If you want to see what the writing looks like, you can use something like Otter.AI to transcribe it for you.

In summary, scripting is a powerful manifestation technique that involves writing down your goals and dreams as if they have already happened, in the present tense

SIGILS:

Sigils are like magic symbols that are used to manifest your desires and goals. Think of them like little power-packed emojis that you can create and use to manifest your wildest dreams. They're like a secret code that you create to communicate with the universe, and they're super easy to make. Just take a word or phrase that represents your desire, and turn it into a symbol. Then, you can carry it with you, put it on your wall, or even tattoo it on your body to remind you of your intention. It's like having your own personal genie in a bottle, but instead of a genie, it's your own personal sigil working hard to make your wishes come true

Creating a sigil is like baking a cake, you have to have the right ingredients and follow the recipe. First, you gotta decide what you want, like really want. It can be anything from a new job to a new love. Write it down in one sentence, and make sure it's something you truly desire. Next, you gotta get rid of all the unnecessary letters, like vowels and repeating letters. Now you're left with the important letters that represent your desire. Take those letters and rearrange them into a symbol that resonates with you. This can be anything from a simple geometric shape to a more complex design. Once you've got your symbol, it's time to charge it. This can be done by meditating on your desire while staring at the symbol, or by using visualization techniques to infuse it with energy. And voila! You've just created your very own sigil. Now, you can carry it with you, put it on your wall, or even tattoo it on your body to remind you of your intention. Just remember, the power of a sigil lies in your belief and focus on it. So, go ahead and create your own sigil, and watch as the universe works its magic to make your wildest dreams come true.

I like to draw sigils on my hand. I know other people that have them tattooed even get them to put on your nail art if you want to be fine with it. I've also done schedules for protection over my bed when I was going through a bad time with certain spirits, and it really really does the trick. Using them to manifest abundance has been new but something that's been working quite successfully for me

So, don't be afraid to dream big, sister. Get clear on what you want and make it happen. And remember, you're in control of your destiny, so don't let anyone tell you otherwise. Now go out there and manifest.

1. **Believe it's possible. You gotta have faith that what you want can happen. If you don't believe it, no one else will either.**

Believing in your dreams and aspirations is a crucial factor in manifesting them. When you have faith that what you desire is possible, you align your thoughts, feelings, and actions towards achieving it. Without this belief, you'll lack the motivation and focus needed to take the necessary steps towards your goal.

Your beliefs act as a filter for your experiences, and if you believe that something is impossible, your mind will filter out any evidence that suggests otherwise. On the other hand, if you have unwavering faith in your dreams, you'll start to notice opportunities and synchronicities that will lead you closer to your goal.

1. **Take action. It's all well and good to sit around visualising and manifesting, but you gotta put in the work too. The universe will help you out, but you gotta meet it halfway.**

If you want something in this life, you gotta put in the work. Sitting around visualizing and manifesting is all well and good, but it ain't gonna get you anywhere if you don't take action. The universe is a powerful thing, but it ain't no genie in a bottle. You gotta meet it halfway.

You wanna be successful? You gotta hustle. You wanna lose weight? You gotta hit the gym. You wanna find love? You gotta put yourself out there. Do you see where I'm going with this? The universe may give you a helping hand, but it ain't gonna do all the work for you.

So, stop dreaming and start doing. Stop waiting for things to happen and make them happen. Stop thinking and start acting. Because let's be real, the universe ain't gonna hand you anything on a silver platter. You gotta go out there and grab it yourself.

In short, visualizing and manifesting are all well and good, but if you want something, you gotta put in the work. The universe may help you out, but you gotta meet it halfway. So, get up, get out, and make it happen. Because, ain't nobody gonna do it for you.

1. **Let go of the outcome. Stop worrying about whether or not it's going to happen. Trust that the universe has your back and let go of the need to control everything.**

You're worrying yourself sick over whether or not things are gonna happen. And let me tell you, that kind of stress ain't good for nobody. So, take a deep breath and let go of the outcome. Trust that the universe has got your back.

You see, when you're constantly fixated on the outcome, you're not living in the present. You're not enjoying the journey. You're not taking the time to appreciate all the little things that happen along the way. And let me tell you, those little things are what make life worth living.

So, stop trying to control everything. Stop trying to micromanage every little thing. Because , that ain't how the universe works. The universe has its own plan. And let me tell you, it's usually way better than the one you have in mind.

In short, stop worrying about the outcome. Trust that the universe has your back and let go of the need to control everything. Enjoy the journey and appreciate the little things. Because , that's what life is all about.

1. **Receive it with grace. When your manifestation comes to fruition, be grateful and receive it with open arms. You deserve it!**

You've been working hard, putting in the effort, and visualizing your manifestation to fruition. And let me tell you, you deserve it. So, when it finally happens, you better receive it with grace.

The Universe has a funny way of surprising us and sometimes what we think we want, isn't what we actually need.

So, instead of being attached to one specific manifestation, approach everything from a neutral stance. Be open to new opportunities and new possibilities. Because let me tell you, the universe is full of endless possibilities. And if you're too attached to one thing, you might miss out on something even better.

You see, when you receive something with grace, it shows the universe that you're grateful. And let me tell you, the universe loves a grateful person. It shows that you're open to receiving more good things in the future.

So, when your manifestation comes to fruition, don't just take it and run. Don't just take it for granted. Stop and appreciate it. Take a moment to reflect on all the hard work you put in to make it happen. And let me tell you, it's going to feel even sweeter.

In short, when your manifestation comes to fruition, receive it with grace. Be grateful for it and show the universe that you're open to receiving more good things.

Once you know what your manifestations are, you understand of course because of the earlier reference in the book that they will be limiting beliefs about these manifestations. Once you've identified them, it's important to look at them closely in order to understand how they're holding you back and what you can do to overcome them. You can do this by understanding the source of the limiting belief, identifying the evidence that contradicts the belief, challenging the belief by asking yourself if it's really true and replacing the limiting belief with a positive and empowering one.

Write down a list of what your manifestations are in one column, and then in the next column I want you to ask why I believe that I cannot have this? In the column next to that I want you to ask, who or what gave me this belief? In the next column, challenge the belief by asking yourself if it's really true. Ask yourself questions like: Is this belief really true? Has this belief ever been true in the past? Is there any evidence that contradicts this belief? And in the next column, Replace the limiting belief with a positive and empowering one. Once you've identified and challenged your limiting belief, it's important to replace it with a positive and empowering one. This will help you to shift your focus from what you can't do, to what you can do.

HOW TO HEAL SCARCITY MENTALITY:

Scarcity mentality is when you're all like, "I don't have enough, I'm not enough, and I'm never going to be enough!" It's like a big black cloud of negativity that just follows you around and sucks the joy out of life. It's like having a little voice in your head that's always telling you that you're never going to have enough, be enough, or do enough. And that voice is a total buzzkill!

Basically, it's a mindset that's all about lack and limitation. You're constantly worried about running out of resources, whether it's money, time, or love. You feel like there's never enough to go around, and you have to hold onto everything tightly, or it'll slip through your fingers. It's like you're living in a desert, and you're always thirsty, but there's never enough water to go around.

And here's the thing, sis, scarcity mentality is a total trap! It keeps you stuck in a cycle of fear and anxiety, and it stops you from living your best life. It's like you're wearing blinders, and you can only see the negative side of things. But guess what? There's a whole world of abundance out there, just waiting for you to tap into it! You just gotta shift your mindset and start believing that there's plenty to go around.

When you're coming from a history of trauma, then scars

to mentality is totally normal. In fact a lot of people have it. Including myself. I'm still healing mine. And treating this in the same way that I did with trying to heal my trauma. I'm trying lots of different methods. Because I find that I can manifest things, but that they can quickly leave. And I believe that that's because they're not going to stay around. So that's the next age of my healing journey. These are some of the things that I've been working for me:

Gratitude:

So, if you want to start manifesting your desires and bringing positive things into your life, start by cultivating a gratitude attitude. Trust me, it's a game-changer.

A scarcity mindset is when you believe that there's never enough to go around. You're always thinking about what you don't have and what you need, instead of being grateful for what you do have. It's like living in a constant state of FOMO (fear of missing out) and feeling like you're constantly missing out on something better. It's a mindset that keeps you stuck in a cycle of never feeling satisfied and always wanting more

People can have a scarcity mindset because they're constantly bombarded with messages that there's not enough to go around. Society teaches us to compete, to constantly strive for more, and to never be satisfied with what we have. It's easy to fall into the trap of thinking that we need more money, more things, and more status to be happy. But let me tell you, that's a recipe for disaster. We're never going to have enough if we keep chasing after something that's always out of reach. It's a mindset that keeps us in a constant state of wanting, but never getting

Here are the top 5 signs that you've got a scarcity mindset:

1. You're always comparing yourself to others and feeling like you're not good enough.
2. You're constantly chasing after the next big thing,

and never feeling satisfied with what you have.

3. You're always looking for ways to get more and more, never feeling like you have enough.

4. You're constantly worried about what you don't have, instead of being grateful for what you do have.

5. You're always in a state of FOMO (fear of missing out) and feeling like you're missing out on something better.

If you're nodding your head to any of these signs, it's time to take a step back and re-evaluate your mindset. Remember, abundance is a choice, and it's time to choose it.

But when we shift our mindset from scarcity to abundance, suddenly everything changes. We stop thinking about what we can get, and start thinking about what we can give. It's that simple, but it's also that powerful.

First of all, let's get one thing straight: gratitude is not just about saying "thank you" when someone holds the door open for you. It's about actively seeking out the good in your life and acknowledging it. It's about being mindful of the present and appreciating what you have, rather than constantly focusing on what you don't have.

But why should you care about any of this? Well, for starters, gratitude has been scientifically proven to improve physical and mental health. It can reduce stress, lower blood pressure, and even improve your immune system. It can also increase your overall satisfaction with life and boost your mood. According to an article on Harvard Health, two bad-ass psychologists, Dr. Robert A. Emmons and Dr. Michael E. McCullough, have been doing real research on gratitude. And let me tell you, they know their stuff! In one study, they had participants write down their thoughts each week on different topics.

One group wrote about things they were grateful for that had occurred during the week. Another group wrote about daily irritations or things that had displeased them, and the third wrote about events that had affected them (with no emphasis on them being positive or negative). After 10 weeks, those who wrote about gratitude were more optimistic and felt better about their lives. And get this, they even exercised more and had fewer visits to physicians than those who focused on sources of aggravation.

Another leading researcher in this field, Dr. Martin E. P. Seligman tested the impact of various positive psychology interventions on 411 people, each compared with a control assignment of writing about early memories. When their week's assignment was to write and personally deliver a letter of gratitude to someone who had never been properly thanked for his or her kindness, participants immediately exhibited a huge increase in happiness scores. This impact was greater than that from any other intervention, with benefits lasting for a month.

Now, let's not get ahead of ourselves, these studies can't prove cause and effect. But most of the studies published on this topic support an association between gratitude and an individual's well-being, so don't be a sceptic. Start being grateful, it's good for you!

But let's be real, the true power of gratitude lies in the way it can change your perspective. When you make a habit of being thankful, you start to see the world differently. Suddenly, those small, everyday moments become just as important as the big, flashy ones. You start to appreciate the little things and find joy in the simple things in life.

And let's not forget the power of gratitude in relationships. Showing appreciation and thankfulness towards those around you can strengthen your bonds and deepen connections. Plus, who doesn't love feeling appreciated?

Working with the universal laws, and manifesting, gratitude is one of the most powerful ways that you can work with the law of attraction. The law of attraction is basically the idea that you can manifest your desires and bring positive things into your life by focusing on positive thoughts and emotions. It's like a magnet, what you put out there comes back to you. And let me tell you, having a gratitude attitude is key to making this law work for you.

When you're constantly thinking about what you're grateful for, you're sending out positive vibes to the universe. You're telling the universe that you're content with what you have and that you're open to receiving more good things. This positive energy attracts more positive things into your life.

On the other hand, when you're constantly focusing on lack and scarcity, you're sending out negative vibes and you'll attract more negative things into your life. It's that simple.

So, if you want to start manifesting your desires and bring positive things into your life, start by cultivating a gratitude attitude. Trust me, it's a game changer.

So, how can you start incorporating gratitude into your life? It's simple! Start a gratitude journal and write down one thing you're thankful for every day. Or make it a point to express appreciation to someone in your life every day. And don't forget to practice self-gratitude too, by acknowledging your own accomplishments and progress.

Here are some things that you can be grateful for:

1. Your ability to laugh at yourself - It's the ultimate sign of self-confidence and self-awareness.
2. Your bed - It's the ultimate sanctuary after a long day.
3. Your friends - They're the ones who have your back, no matter what.
4. Your freedom - Whether it's the freedom to speak

your mind or the freedom to make your own choices, it's a precious thing.

5. Your hobbies - They bring joy and fulfilment to your life.

6. The ability to learn and grow - Life is a journey, and every day is an opportunity to learn something new.

7. The power of choice - Every day you have the power to make your own choices, and that's something to be grateful for.

8. The beauty of nature - From sunset to a flower, nature's beauty is a constant reminder of the world's wonder.

9. Your job: even if you hate it, it allows you to pay for the things that you need in life and even though that can suck sometimes in the way that has to come about, being grateful for this will really make all the difference.

10. Your pets or animals in your life. Whether they be furry or scaly, these little mofos bring a lot of joy to all of our lives.

In short, gratitude is not just a sappy, boring concept. It's a secret weapon to living your best life, improving your health, and strengthening your relationships. So don't be afraid to embrace it, and start feeling the power of gratitude today.

HYPNOSIS:

The subconscious mind is responsible for driving our thoughts, emotions, and behaviours, and it's constantly working behind the scenes to ensure our survival and well-being. However, much of what the subconscious mind has learned and stored over time may not be in our best interest. It could be outdated beliefs, self-sabotaging behaviours, or negative thought patterns that limit us from achieving our full potential.

To make real and lasting changes in our lives, we need to access and reprogram the subconscious mind. This is where therapies like hypnotherapy can be incredibly helpful. CBT works by identifying negative thought patterns and behaviours and replacing them. Through this process, you can retrain their subconscious minds to think, feel, and act in a way that aligns with their goals and desires.

While it's important to acknowledge and work through difficult emotions and past traumas, we don't have to be held back by them. By understanding and reprogramming our subconscious minds, we can break free from limiting beliefs and behaviours and create the life we truly want. Hypnosis is an excellent tool for this process, as it provides a safe and supportive space to explore and transform the subconscious mind.

Hypnosis is a state of mind where you're super relaxed and focused, and your subconscious mind is more open to suggestions than usual. And let's be real, it's the subconscious mind that's really running the show, so that's why hypnosis is a big deal. It's like reprogramming your brain to work in your favour. And that's why hypnosis is a winner because you can train your brain to work for you instead of against you. You can find good hypnotists through Google, social media or on Woo Woo. Make sure you read the reviews first!

There are also ways to do self Hypnosis, with lots of YouTube videos, and even apps that offer this as a subscription service. Which is what I've been doing. I've been loving the app get Grace, which has lots of Hypnosis on there. And some of them you can actually play whilst you sleep, so that they reprogram your brain as you dream.

AFFIRMATIONS:

Oh my God, I LOVE affirmations so much. When I first heard about them, I never thought it would be something I do. I thought it was cheesy and repetitive, and only really insecure people did them. That is of course because I was coming from a negative mindset,around something that I've never tried before. But in a lot of the books that I read that I admired, the authors and a lot of the people I admired mentioned that they did them. So I thought, well if they've done that, and they're leading a life that I would like to lead, then I need to try them too. It's another really powerful way to reprogram the brain.

Let's talk about what affirmations actually are. They're positive statements that you repeat to yourself, usually daily, to reinforce a belief or mindset you want to cultivate. And here's the thing: your brain is like a sponge, always soaking up information and experiences. So when you repeat affirmations, you're essentially giving your brain a new script to follow, one that's more aligned with your goals and aspirations.

There's some serious science backing up their effectiveness. Studies have shown that affirmations can help reduce stress, improve self-esteem, and even alleviate symptoms of depression. And when you think about it, it makes sense. If you're constantly telling yourself positive things, you're going to start believing them, and that can have a profound impact on your mood and overall well-being.

Affirmations work with the brain in several ways. When you repeat a positive affirmation, you are essentially sending a message to your brain that reinforces a particular belief or mindset. This repetition can create new neural pathways in your brain, making it easier for you to think and act in alignment with the affirmation.

Additionally, affirmations can help to counteract negative self-talk, which can be a significant source of stress and anxiety. By replacing negative self-talk with positive affirmations, you can reprogram your brain to focus on the positive aspects of your life, which can help to reduce stress and improve your overall mood.

Moreover, affirmations can also help to build your self-esteem and self-confidence. When you repeat affirmations that focus on your strengths and positive qualities, you start to believe in yourself more, which can have a ripple effect in all areas of your life.

An exercise for you:

1. Create a table
2. Write down five of your biggest dreams
3. Next, write down all of the reasons that you believe that you can't get them
4. Next to each belief I want you to write down if you have any evidence of why this reason it's true (most likely it isn't)
5. Next to that, I want you to write down an affirmation to say why you can get it

This is going to become your affirmation. And I want you to repeat them all day every day. Specifically as well before you're going to bed because that's when the brain is in theatre waves wind at the subconscious is most suggestible.

Here are some of my favourite affirmations in different categories in case that helps you:

Affirmations for abundance:

1. I am a magnet for abundance and prosperity, and I welcome it into my life with open arms.
2. Money flows easily and effortlessly to me, and I always have more than enough to meet my needs and desires.
3. I am grateful for the abundance that surrounds me, and I always find ways to share my blessings with others.
4. I trust in the universe to provide for me, and I know that everything I need will come to me at the perfect time and in the perfect way.
5. I am worthy of abundance and success, and I trust in my own abilities to create a life of prosperity and abundance.

Affirmations for a positive mindset:

1. I choose to focus on the positive in all situations, and I trust that everything will work out for my highest good.
2. I am capable of overcoming any challenges that come my way, and I trust in my ability to find solutions and grow from every experience.
3. I release all negative thoughts and emotions, and I choose to fill my mind with positive, uplifting thoughts that inspire and motivate me.
4. I am worthy of love, success, and happiness, and I choose to believe in myself and my ability to achieve my goals and dreams.
5. I am grateful for all the blessings in my life, and I choose to approach every day with a sense of wonder, joy, and gratitude.

Affirmations to help with anxiety:

1. I am safe and protected, and I trust that everything is going to be okay.

2. I release all fear and worry, and I choose to focus on the present moment with a calm and peaceful mind.
3. I trust in my ability to handle any situation that comes my way, and I have faith that I can overcome any challenges.
4. I am surrounded by love and support, and I know that I am not alone in my struggles.
5. I am capable of finding inner peace and calm, and I choose to focus on my breath and relax my body in times of stress and anxiety.

Affirmations to help with a scarcity mindset:

1. I trust that there is always enough abundance and prosperity to go around, and I am open to receiving it in all areas of my life.
2. I release all limiting beliefs around scarcity and lack, and I choose to focus on abundance, gratitude, and possibility.
3. I am worthy of wealth and success, and I trust in my ability to create a life of prosperity and abundance for myself.
4. I choose to see abundance all around me, and I am grateful for the blessings in my life, no matter how small.
5. I release all fear and anxiety around money and resources, and I trust that the universe is always conspiring to support me in manifesting my desires.

I've also been loving subliminal affirmations, which are positive messages that are delivered to your subconscious mind at a level below your conscious awareness. Subliminal messages can be delivered in a variety of formats, including visual images, spoken words, and even music or sounds. These messages are designed to bypass your critical thinking and go straight to your subconscious, which is where many of your beliefs and behaviours are rooted.

One of the key benefits of listening to subliminal affirmations is that they can help to reprogram your subconscious mind with positive, empowering beliefs. Because subliminal messages bypass your conscious mind, they can be very effective in helping to change deep-seated beliefs and behaviours that may be holding you back. For example, if you have a belief that you're not good enough to achieve your goals, subliminal affirmations can help to reprogram your subconscious mind with positive messages that empower and motivate you to take action.

Another benefit of listening to subliminal affirmations is that they can help to create a sense of calm and relaxation. Many subliminal recordings are designed to help you relax and let go of stress and anxiety, which can be beneficial for your overall well-being.

Overall, subliminal affirmations can be a powerful tool for reprogramming your subconscious mind with positive beliefs and empowering messages. While they may not be a magic solution to all of your problems, they can be a helpful complement to other personal development practices like meditation, visualization, and positive thinking.

Subliminal affirmations can be found on various platforms, including podcasts and YouTube videos. Many creators and producers make subliminal affirmations accessible to everyone to help them improve their lives and well-being. Here's how you can find them:

1. On podcasts: You can find subliminal affirmations on podcasting platforms like Apple Podcasts, Spotify, and Google Podcasts. Search for keywords like "subliminal affirmations," "self-improvement," or "positive thinking" to find relevant shows. Once you find a show that interests you, listen to the episodes to see if they include subliminal affirmations that

align with your goals and values.

2. On YouTube: YouTube is another great source of subliminal affirmations. You can search for specific keywords and phrases related to your goals, such as "subliminal affirmations for confidence" or "subliminal affirmations for abundance." There are many channels on YouTube that specialise in subliminal affirmations, and you can find a variety of videos to choose from. You can also read the comments and reviews to see if others have found the affirmations helpful.

When you find a podcast or video that includes subliminal affirmations, make sure to listen or watch them consistently to get the full benefit. It's also important to remember that subliminal affirmations are not a substitute for professional help if you are dealing with mental health issues. If you're struggling with anxiety, depression, or other mental health concerns, it's important to seek the help of a trained mental health professional.

CHAPTER 8: OH MY STARS - LET'S TALK ASTROLOGY!

In a world where we're bombarded with messages telling us who we should be, it can be damn hard to figure out who we actually are. But astrology? That's a tool that can help you cut through all the noise and find your true purpose and identity.

Oh, astrology? It's just the coolest thing ever. It's like a cosmic map of the universe that helps us understand ourselves and our place in the world.

Basically, astrology is the study of the stars and the planets and their influence on our lives. It's been around for centuries, and it's used by people all over the world to gain insight into their personalities, relationships, and future.

At the heart of astrology is the natal chart, which is like a snapshot of the sky at the exact moment and place you were born. It takes into account the position of the sun, moon, planets, and stars, and it reveals a ton of information about your unique personality traits, strengths, challenges, and life path.

You see, your natal chart is like a blueprint of your soul. It's a snapshot of the cosmos at the exact moment and place you were born, and it holds clues to your unique talents, passions, and challenges. It's like having your own personal roadmap to self-discovery.

When you dive into your natal chart and explore the various components - your sun, moon, and rising signs, your planets and houses - you start to uncover a deeper understanding of yourself. You start to see patterns and themes in your life, and you gain insights into why you might be drawn to certain careers, hobbies, or relationships.

And let me tell you - there's nothing more empowering than knowing who you are and what you're here to do. When you have a clear sense of your purpose and your identity, you can navigate the world with confidence and clarity. You can make decisions that are aligned with your true self, and you can let go of all the expectations and pressures that don't serve you.

So if you're feeling lost or uncertain, turn to astrology. It might just be the key to unlocking your true potential and finding your place in this crazy world.

I'm no expert astrologer. I mean, I know a thing or two about the stars and the planets, and I love to read horoscopes as much as the next gal. But when it comes to the nitty-gritty details of a natal chart? I'll leave that to the pros.

That being said, I do have a genuine interest in astrology, and I've picked up some tidbits along the way. So if you want to chat about your sun sign or your rising sign or your Mercury retrograde mishaps, I'm your gal. I can give you some insight and maybe even a few sassy quips to brighten your day.

But, if you really want to go deep and unlock the full potential of your natal chart, I highly recommend booking a session with a professional astrologer. These folks have spent years studying the stars and the planets, and they have a level of expertise that I can only dream of.

An astrologer can give you a comprehensive reading of your natal chart, taking into account all the intricate details and nuances. They can help you understand your strengths and challenges, your purpose and your path. And they can do it all with a level of accuracy and insight that will leave you feeling truly seen and understood.

First things first, let's talk about the zodiac signs. You know 'em, you love 'em, but do you really know what they mean? Each sign has its own unique personality traits and quirks, so get ready to dive deep into the cosmic world of astrology.

SUN, MOON AND RISING SIGNS:

Let me tell you about the holy trinity of the natal chart - the sun, moon, and rising signs.

if you've never really felt like your sun sign describes you, don't worry - you're not alone. In fact, it's pretty common for people to feel like their sun sign doesn't fully capture who they are. And you know why? It's because you're so much more than just one sign.

You see, astrology is a complex system that takes into account not just your sun sign, but also your moon sign, rising sign, and all the planets and houses in your natal chart. Each of these components adds a layer of complexity to your astrological profile, and they all work together to create a unique, multifaceted portrait of who you are.

So maybe your sun sign is a fiery Aries, but your moon sign is a sensitive Cancer. Maybe your rising sign is a grounded Taurus, but your Venus is in wild and rebellious Aquarius. All of these components work together to create a beautiful, complex mosaic of your astrological identity.

And here's the thing - your moon sign, in particular, is a powerful force in your natal chart. It represents your emotional world, your inner self, and your subconscious desires. It's the part of you that you might not show to the world, but that drives so much of your behaviour and decision-making.

So if you've never really identified with your sun sign, don't fret. It just means that there's so much more to you than meets the eye. Take some time to explore your moon sign and all the other components of your natal chart.

First up, we have the sun sign. This bad boy represents your core identity, your ego, and your overall personality. It's the sign that you're probably most familiar with, and it's what most people mean when they say their zodiac sign. So, if you're a Leo, you're all about that confidence, creativity, and dramatic flair. A Pisces? Get ready for some dreamy, intuitive vibes.

Next, we have the moon sign. This baby represents your emotional world, your inner self, and your subconscious desires. It's the yin to the sun sign's yang, and it's what gives you depth and complexity. So, if you're a Cancer moon, you're all about those feelings - nurturing, empathetic, and maybe a little moody. A Scorpio moon? Get ready for some intense, passionate emotions.

And last but not least, we have the rising sign, also known as the ascendant. This bad boy represents your outward self, your first impression, and your physical appearance. It's what people first notice about you, and it can affect the way you come across to others. So, if you're a Sagittarius rising, you're all about that adventurous, outgoing energy. A Virgo rising? Get ready for some detail-oriented, perfectionist vibes.

Now, here's the thing - all three of these signs work together to create a unique, complex portrait of who you are. It's not enough to just know your sun sign - you gotta dive deep and explore all aspects of your natal chart. And hey, even if you don't fully believe in astrology, it's still a fun way to learn more about yourself and the people around you. So go forth and embrace your sun, moon, and rising signs. It's all a part of your cosmic journey.

MERCURY'S IN LEMONADE AGAIN:

When planets go retrograde, it's like the universe is playing a cosmic game of twister! But don't worry, I'll break it down for you.

When a planet goes retrograde, it appears to be moving backwards in the sky. It's not actually doing that, mind you - it's just an optical illusion caused by the relative position of the planet and the Earth. But astrologers pay attention to these retrogrades because they can have a big impact on our lives.

Mercury retrograde is probably the most famous retrograde, and it happens a few times a year. When Mercury goes retrograde, it's like the communication planet is going on vacation - everything from technology to transportation can go haywire. So be prepared for missed appointments, lost keys, and flaky friends during this time.

Venus retrograde is a little less frequent, but it can be just as impactful. When Venus goes retrograde, it's like the planet of love and beauty is taking a nap. This can be a great time to reflect on your relationships and figure out what you really want, but it's not a good time to start a new romance or make any major beauty changes.

Mars retrograde is another biggie, and it only happens once every couple of years. When Mars goes retrograde, it's like the planet of action and energy is stuck in traffic. You might feel a bit sluggish or unmotivated during this time, but it can also be a great time to reassess your goals and make sure you're on the right path.

And those are just a few of the retrogrades! Every planet has its own unique energy and impact, so there's always something astrologically sassy happening in the cosmos. So keep an eye on those retrogrades, , and don't let them trip you up - they're just a cosmic reminder to slow down and take a breather.

It's easy to get caught up in all the fear and drama that can surround retrogrades. But let me tell you, the planets might have their own power, but you have your own power too.

Your personal power comes from within, and it's something that no planet can take away from you. You get to decide how you react to the energy of a retrograde or any other astrological event.

So don't let those retrogrades get you down. You can still accomplish amazing things and manifest your dreams no matter what the planets are doing. In fact, some astrologers believe that retrogrades can actually be a time of great growth and transformation if you approach them with the right mindset.

Remember, astrology is a tool for self-awareness and empowerment, not a way to predict your fate. So use it to tap into your own personal power and create the life you want! The planets might be doing their thing, but you're the one in the driver's seat of your own destiny.

THE DIFFERENT SIGNS:

Aries? They're the fiery, headstrong leaders of the zodiac. Taurus? The bulls of the group, stubborn but oh-so-steady. Gemini? The social butterflies who are always down for a good time. Cancer? The emotional crabs who wear their hearts on their sleeves. Leo? The confident, attention-seeking lions who always steal the show.

Virgo? The perfectionists who always have their sh*t together. Libra? The charming diplomats who just want everyone to get along. Scorpio? The mysterious and passionate creatures who are not to be messed with. Sagittarius? The adventurous, free-spirited archers who live for the thrill of the chase.

Capricorn? The hardworking, ambitious goats who will stop at nothing to reach the top. Aquarius? The unconventional, eccentric geniuses who always think outside the box. And last but not least, Pisces? The dreamy, intuitive fish who are always in touch with their emotions.

Now, let's talk about horoscopes. Sure, they may seem like generic predictions based on your sign, but let's be real - we all secretly love reading them. Whether you're checking your daily, weekly, or monthly horoscope, it's a fun way to see what the stars have in store for you. Just don't take them too seriously, okay?

And finally, we can't talk about astrology without mentioning Mercury Retrograde. You know the drill - technology glitches, communication breakdowns, and general chaos. But fear not, my friends. Just take a deep breath, double-check your plans, and remember that it's only temporary. Plus, it gives us all an excuse to blame the stars for our problems.

What does your north node and south node mean in astrology?

The North Node and South Node are points in a person's birth chart that are calculated based on their date, time, and place of birth. These points are significant in astrology because they represent areas of growth and challenges in a person's life, and they are often used to help identify a person's life purpose and direction. The North Node represents the things that a person is meant to work towards and develop in their life, while the South Node represents the things that a person has already mastered or become too reliant on.

In astrology, the North Node and South Node are points in the sky that are directly opposite each other. The North Node, also known as the "Dragon's Head," represents the future and the things we are meant to embrace in this lifetime. It symbolises the qualities and traits we need to develop and cultivate in order to fulfill our destiny and reach our full potential. The South Node, also known as the "Dragon's Tail," represents the past and the things we need to let go of in order to move forward. It represents the traits and patterns we have carried over from previous lifetimes that are no longer serving us and that we need to release in order to grow.

The North Node is often associated with new beginnings, growth, and forward movement, while the South Node is associated with the past, comfort, and familiarity. The North Node represents the challenges we need to face in order to grow and evolve, while the South Node represents the things that come easily to us and that we tend to rely on.

In a birth chart, the positions of the North and South Nodes can give us insight into the lessons and challenges we will face in this lifetime and the qualities we need to cultivate in order to fulfil our destiny. They can also give us insight into the things we need to let go of in order to move forward and grow.

To use your North Node in order to become a better person, you can focus on developing the qualities and characteristics associated with your North Node. This may involve exploring new activities and experiences that challenge you to grow and learn, and seeking out opportunities to practice the skills and traits associated with your North Node.

It may also be helpful to consider the sign and house placement of your North Node, as these can provide additional insight into the specific areas of your life where you are meant to focus your growth and development. For example, if your North Node is in the sign of Leo and the 10th house, you may be meant to focus on developing your leadership skills and taking on more responsibility in your career.

Ultimately, the key to using your North Node to become a better person is to embrace your unique path and work to become the person you are meant to be. This may involve facing challenges and making difficult choices, but it can also bring great fulfilment and purpose to your life.

The south node in a birth chart is often associated with past experiences and patterns of behaviour that may be holding you back in your current life. It can be helpful to understand the energies and themes associated with your south node in order to identify any negative patterns or habits that you may want to work on releasing or transforming.

One way to use your south node in your birth chart to grow is to reflect on the qualities and characteristics associated with it, and consider how you can use these energies in a more positive and constructive way. For example, if your south node is in a sign that is associated with creativity, you may want to explore ways to tap into your creative side and use it to express yourself or solve problems.

It can also be helpful to work with a therapist or astrologer to gain a deeper understanding of your south node and how it may be impacting your life. This can provide valuable insights and guidance as you work on transforming any negative patterns or habits associated with your south node.

Remember that personal growth is a lifelong process, and it's okay to take small steps and make mistakes along the way. With awareness and effort, you can use your south node as a tool for growth and transformation.

The first house:

The first house in astrology is also known as the Ascendant or the Rising sign. It is the house that was rising on the eastern horizon at the time of your birth, and it is considered one of the most important houses in a natal chart.

The first house represents the beginning of the natural zodiac, and it is associated with your self-image, your physical appearance, and your sense of self. It also represents your initial responses to new situations and experiences, and it can indicate how you come across to others.

The first house is ruled by the planet Mars, and its sign is Aries. If you have a strong Aries influence in your first house, you may be seen as confident and assertive, with a natural tendency to take charge and lead. If you have a strong influence from the planet Mars, you may be more action-oriented and energetic, with a strong drive to succeed.

Overall, the first house is an important factor in understanding your personality and how you present yourself to the world.

The second house:

The second house in astrology is associated with material possessions, finances, and values. It represents your resources and what you value in life, including your sense of self-worth and self-esteem.

The second house is also associated with your personal possessions, including your material possessions and your physical body. It can indicate how you acquire and manage your resources, as well as your attitudes towards money and material possessions.

The second house is ruled by the planet Venus, and its sign is Taurus. If you have a strong Taurus influence in your second house, you may be more security-oriented and may place a high value on material possessions. If you have a strong influence from Venus, you may be more artistic and sensual, with a strong appreciation for beauty.

Overall, the second house is an important factor in understanding your relationship with material possessions and your values in life.

The third house:

The third house in astrology is associated with communication, learning, and the mind. It represents your mental abilities and how you process and communicate information, as well as your relationships with siblings, neighbours, and other close relationships.

The fourth house:

The fourth house in astrology is associated with home, family, and the past. It represents your emotional foundation, your sense of security and belonging, and your early upbringing.

The fourth house is also associated with your home and family life, including your relationship with your parents and your home environment. It can indicate your sense of security and your emotional stability.

The fourth house is ruled by the Moon, and its sign is Cancer. If you have a strong Cancer influence in your fourth house, you may be more emotional and sensitive, with a strong need for security and a close connection to your family. If you have a strong influence from the Moon, you may be more intuitive and nurturing, with a strong need for emotional stability.

Overall, the fourth house is an important factor in understanding your emotional foundation and your relationships with your family and home environment**.**

The fifth house:

The fifth house in astrology is associated with creativity, self-expression, and romance. It represents your creative abilities and your ability to express yourself, as well as your sense of fun and enjoyment.

The fifth house is also associated with romance and relationships, and it can indicate your ability to form strong, meaningful connections with others. It is also associated with children and pregnancy, and it can indicate your potential to create and nurture new life.

The fifth house is ruled by the Sun, and its sign is Leo. If you have a strong Leo influence in your fifth house, you may be more confident and self-expressive, with a strong need to be seen and heard. If you have a strong influence from the Sun, you may be more radiant and charismatic, with a strong need to shine and be recognised.

Overall, the fifth house is an important factor in understanding your creative abilities and your relationships with others.

The sixth house:

The sixth house in astrology is associated with work, health, and service. It represents your daily routine and the tasks and responsibilities that you take on, as well as your physical health and well-being.

The sixth house is also associated with your job or career, and it can indicate your work ethic and your attitude towards work. It is also associated with your ability to take care of yourself and maintain your health, as well as your relationships with pets and other animals.

The sixth house is ruled by the planet Mercury, and its sign is Virgo. If you have a strong Virgo influence in your sixth house, you may be more organised and detail-oriented, with a strong work ethic and a tendency to be perfectionistic. If you have a strong influence from Mercury, you may be more communicative and analytical, with strong problem-solving skills.

Overall, the sixth house is an important factor in understanding your work and health habits, as well as your relationships with others.

The seventh house:

The seventh house in astrology is associated with relationships, partnerships, and marriage. It represents your one-on-one relationships, including romantic relationships and business partnerships, and it can indicate your ability to form strong, lasting bonds with others.

The seventh house is also associated with your sense of balance and fairness, and it can indicate your ability to compromise and work with others towards common goals. It is also associated with your public image and how you present yourself to the world in your relationships.

The seventh house is ruled by the planet Venus, and its sign is Libra. If you have a strong Libra influence in your seventh house, you may be more diplomatic and fair-minded, with a strong desire for harmony in your relationships. If you have a strong influence from Venus, you may be more artistic and sensual, with a strong appreciation for beauty.

Overall, the seventh house is an important factor in understanding your relationships with others and your ability to form partnerships.

The eighth house

The eighth house in astrology is associated with death, transformation, and the occult. It represents your deeper, hidden side, including your unconscious desires and motivations, as well as your ability to transform and regenerate.

The eighth house is also associated with shared resources, including money and assets that are shared with others, such as a spouse or business partner. It can indicate your ability to manage and make the most of shared resources, as well as your attitudes towards power and control in your relationships.

The eighth house is ruled by the planet Pluto, and its sign is Scorpio. If you have a strong Scorpio influence in your eighth house, you may be more intense and passionate, with a strong desire for transformation and regeneration. If you have a strong influence from Pluto, you may be more powerful and transformative, with a strong ability to overcome obstacles and make changes in your life.

Overall, the eighth house is an important factor in understanding your deeper, unconscious motivations and your ability to transform and regenerate.

The ninth house

The ninth house in astrology is associated with higher learning, philosophy, and spirituality. It represents your broadening of horizons and your search for meaning and understanding, as well as your ability to see the bigger picture and think globally.

The ninth house is also associated with long-distance travel and foreign cultures, and it can indicate your willingness to explore and learn about new places and ideas. It is also associated with your beliefs and values, and it can indicate your ability to think critically and form your own opinions.

The ninth house is ruled by the planet Jupiter, and its sign is Sagittarius. If you have a strong Sagittarius influence in your ninth house, you may be more curious and open-minded, with a strong desire for knowledge and understanding. If you have a strong influence from Jupiter, you may be more optimistic and expansive, with a strong ability to see the big picture and think globally.

Overall, the ninth house is an important factor in understanding your search for meaning and understanding, as well as your ability to think critically and form your own opinions.

The tenth house

The tenth house in astrology is associated with career, status, and public reputation. It represents your place in the world and your sense of purpose, as well as your professional goals and aspirations.

The tenth house is also associated with authority and leadership, and it can indicate your ability to take charge and achieve success in your career. It is also associated with your public image and how you are perceived by others in your professional life.

The tenth house is ruled by the planet Saturn, and its sign is Capricorn. If you have a strong Capricorn influence in your tenth house, you may be more ambitious and disciplined, with a strong drive to succeed and a tendency to be hard-working and responsible. If you have a strong influence from Saturn, you may be more practical and grounded, with a strong sense of responsibility and a tendency to be disciplined and organised.

Overall, the tenth house is an important factor in understanding your career goals and your place in the world, as well as your public reputation and image.

The eleventh house

The eleventh house in astrology is associated with friendships, social connections, and group activities. It represents your connections to your community and your ability to work with others towards common goals, as well as your hopes and wishes for the future.

The eleventh house is also associated with your sense of purpose and your personal goals, and it can indicate your ability to achieve success and make a positive impact in the world. It is also associated with your sense of belonging and your ability to connect with others.

The eleventh house is ruled by the planet Uranus, and its sign is Aquarius. If you have a strong Aquarius influence in your eleventh house, you may be more independent and innovative, with a strong desire for social justice and equality. If you have a strong influence from Uranus, you may be more unconventional and rebellious, with a strong need for freedom and autonomy.

Overall, the eleventh house is an important factor in understanding your relationships with others and your sense of purpose and direction in life.

The twelfth house

The twelfth house in astrology is associated with the unconscious, spirituality, and the past. It represents your subconscious mind and your innermost thoughts and feelings, as well as your sense of spirituality and connection to a higher power.

The twelfth house is also associated with endings, and it can indicate your ability to let go of the past and move on to new beginnings. It is also associated with self-undoing and self-sabotage, and it can indicate your unconscious fears and insecurities that may hold you back.

The twelfth house is ruled by the planet Neptune, and its sign is Pisces. If you have a strong Pisces influence in your twelfth house, you may be more intuitive and spiritual, with a strong connection to your unconscious mind and a tendency to be empathetic and compassionate. If you have a strong influence from Neptune, you may be more imaginative and artistic, with a strong connection to the spiritual realm and a tendency to be dreamy and otherworldly.

Overall, the twelfth house is an important factor in understanding your unconscious mind, your spirituality, and your ability to let go of the past and move on to new beginnings.

There is so much more to astrology than what we can cover in just a few paragraphs. But don't worry, I've got you covered with some book recommendations that will take you deeper into the magical world of astrology.

First up, we've got "The Only Astrology Book You'll Ever Need" by Joanna Martine Woolfolk. This book is a classic and for good reason. It's a comprehensive guide to astrology that covers everything from birth charts to compatibility to moon phases. If you're looking for a book that will give you a solid foundation in astrology, this is the one.

Next, we've got "Astrology for the Soul" by Jan Spiller. This book focuses on the North Node and South Node in your birth chart, which represent your soul's purpose and past life experiences. If you're looking for a book that will help you tap into your deeper spiritual purpose, this is the one for you.

For those of you interested in exploring the intersection of astrology and psychology, check out "The Inner Sky" by Steven Forrest. This book delves into the psychological meanings behind each planet and aspect in your birth chart. It's a great resource for understanding yourself on a deeper level.

Finally, if you're interested in the intersection of astrology and tarot, check out "Astrology for Real Life" by Theresa Reed. This book combines astrology and tarot to help you understand your birth chart and life path. It's perfect for those who want to dive deeper into both of these magical practices.

CHAPTER 9:
WITCH, PLEASE!

Witchcraft has been around for longer than you can say "Abracadabra." In ancient times, people would practice various forms of magic and witchcraft as a way to connect with the natural world and honour their gods and goddesses.

I always found it amusing that I had a sense of psychic ability and a witchy energy about me. However, I never considered myself to be a full-fledged witch until recently. After discovering a plethora of books and definitions about what it truly means to be a witch, I finally identified with it in a powerful way.

Embracing my witchy identity has done wonders for my confidence. It's like I've found a missing piece of myself that was always there, but I never fully acknowledged it. I'm no longer afraid to let my inner magic shine and guide me on my path.

I've heard it all when it comes to magic. Some folks think it's a free-for-all where anything goes, including black magic to exact revenge and cause chaos. And hey, if that's their thing, then more power to them. But let me tell you, everything comes with a price, especially when you're messing with dark forces.

As for me, I stick to the bright side of magic. White magic, baby! I use it to help myself feel better and to spread some positivity in this world. I've been on the other side of the fence before, dabbling in some not-so-good magic, and let me tell you, the consequences were not pretty. It's like they say, "what goes around, comes around."

So I'll leave the black magic to those who want to play with fire. I'll stick to my white magic and sleep easy at night knowing that I'm not attracting any negative energy. Plus, there's something truly empowering about using magic for good.

So here I am, proudly embracing my witchiness and all the wonderful things it brings with it. And the best part is, I know there's a whole community of like-minded individuals out there who are cheering me on every step of the way.

So back to the old times, and as Christianity spread, the church began to view witches as a threat to their power, and the infamous witch hunts of the Middle Ages began.

During the witch hunts, thousands of people, mostly women, were accused of practicing witchcraft and were burned at the stake, hanged, or tortured until they confessed. It wasn't until the 20th century that witchcraft began to be viewed in a more positive light, with the rise of Wicca and other neo-pagan movements.

Today, witchcraft is a diverse and thriving community, with practitioners from all walks of life and all corners of the world. Whether you're a solitary witch or part of a coven, there's no denying the power and beauty of witchcraft.

What is the witch wound?

It's the collective trauma and fear that has been passed down for generations regarding witchcraft and anything that falls outside the norm. Back in the day, witches were burned at the stake and persecuted for their beliefs and practices, and that trauma has been passed down from generation to generation.

The witch wound can manifest in many ways, from a fear of being seen as different or a fear of speaking your truth, to a lack of self-confidence and feeling like you need to conform to society's expectations. It can also show up as a resistance to magic and spirituality, or a feeling of shame or guilt around anything that falls outside of the "norm."

But here's the thing, we can heal the witch wound. By embracing our inner witch and tapping into our magic and spirituality, we can break the cycle of fear and trauma and start living our best lives. We can stand in our power, speak our truth, and embrace all the parts of ourselves that make us unique and magical. So let's ditch the witch wound and embrace our inner witches because there's nothing more powerful than a woman who knows her magic.

Let's get real about the witch wound and its connection to feminism. Society has put women in a box for far too long, telling us to play small and stay in our place. And that's exactly what the witch wound is all about. Many of the witches who were persecuted and burned at the stake were women, and it was a form of gendercide. It's a painful part of history, but it's important to acknowledge and confront it.

But here's the thing, being a witch is a powerful way to reclaim that lost power and embrace your inner feminist. It's a way of saying, "I refuse to be silenced or oppressed any longer." It's about tapping into your innate power, connecting with a higher power, and embracing your true self.

And let's not forget that there are so many different types of witchcraft out there, each rooted in different cultures and traditions. By exploring the witchcraft that resonates with your heritage and ancestry, you can connect with your roots and ancestors in a deep and meaningful way. There's a huge power in that, and it can be a powerful tool for self-discovery and healing. So go ahead, embrace your inner witch, reconnect with your heritage, and claim your power.

Here are five sassy ways to overcome the witch wound and

embrace your inner magic:

1. Own your magic! Stop hiding and start shining. Embrace your unique gifts, whether it's your intuition, your creativity, or your ability to manifest your dreams. Don't be afraid to show off your magic, because that's what makes you special.

2. Surround yourself with other witches and like-minded folks! Find a community that supports and uplifts you. Whether it's joining a coven, attending a spiritual retreat, or just finding a group of like-minded friends, being around other magical people can help you feel seen, heard, and validated.

3. Practice self-care! Take care of your mind, body, and spirit. Whether it's taking a bath with your favourite crystals, meditating, or practicing yoga, find ways to nurture yourself and connect with your inner magic.

4. Educate yourself! Learn about the history of witchcraft and the different traditions and practices that resonate with you. Read books, attend workshops, and do your research. The more you know, the more empowered you'll feel.

5. Trust yourself! You are the ultimate authority on your own magic. Don't let anyone else tell you what's right or wrong when it comes to your spiritual path. Trust your intuition, listen to your inner voice, and follow your heart. You've got this.

When you step into witchdom, you are claiming your power and aligning with your true self and a higher power. It's a truly powerful thing because it means you are taking ownership of your life and your destiny. You're saying, "I am in control, and I am going to set my own agenda."

But let's be clear, witchcraft isn't about hurting people or manipulating situations to get what you want. It's about using your innate power and energy to manifest positive changes in your life and in the world around you. As long as you're not causing harm, there's nothing wrong with harnessing your magic and embracing your inner witch.

In fact, stepping into witchdom can be one of the most empowering things you do for yourself. It means letting go of society's expectations and norms, and instead embracing your true self and all that makes you unique. It means tapping into your intuition and connecting with a higher power, and trusting that you have the power to create the life you want. So go ahead, and claim your power as a witch. Embrace your magic, align with your true self, and let your light shine bright!

Did you know about the different types of witches?

First up, we've got the kitchen witch. These witches specialise in cooking up potions and spells using ingredients found in their kitchen. They're like the Martha Stewart of the witchcraft world, whipping up everything from love potions to protection spells with ease.

Next, we've got the green witch. These witches have a deep connection to nature and use plants, herbs, and flowers in their spells and rituals. They're like the ultimate gardeners, creating beautiful and magical gardens filled with herbs and flowers that can be used for everything from healing to divination.

Then there's the cosmic witch. These witches use astrology, tarot, and other divination tools to tap into the universe's energy and create powerful spells and rituals. They're like the ultimate cosmic surfers, riding the waves of the universe and harnessing its energy for their own purposes.

Last but not least, we've got the eclectic witch. These witches don't follow any particular path or tradition, instead, they pick and choose what works for them from a variety of different sources. They're like the ultimate mixologists, creating their own unique brew of witchcraft by blending together different traditions, practices, and beliefs.

So there you have it, my witchy friend! Whether you're a kitchen witch, green witch, cosmic witch, or eclectic witch, there's no denying the power and beauty of witchcraft. So grab your broomstick and let your inner witch fly!

A LIL' MAGICK...

Humans from different cultures and generations have always had an innate connection to the spiritual world, and have explored it through different magickal practices. But let's get one thing straight, Magick is not the same as magic that you see on stage. We're talking about something much deeper and more meaningful here.

Ceremonial magick is rooted in divine tradition. It requires the presence of a pious figure, such as a priest, priestess, or shaman, to connect with the spiritual world. This type of magick has been practised for generations and is deeply rooted in history and tradition. It's all about connecting with the divine and harnessing its power to manifest change in the world around us.

Now, let's talk about celestial magick. This form of manifestation exists at the intersection of the terrestrial and cosmic realms. Astrology is a perfect example of celestial magick. By studying the positions of the stars and planets, we can tap into the energy of the cosmos and use it to manifest our desires.

And let's not forget natural magick. This type of magick uses the power of nature, using herbs, candles, crystals, and stones to direct energy through spell work. It's all about harnessing the energy of the earth and its natural elements to create change in our lives. Whether you're burning sage to clear negative energy, or carrying a crystal for protection, natural magick is a powerful tool for manifestation. So go ahead and explore the many different forms of magick out there. You never know what kind of spiritual growth and manifestation you might uncover.

Let me give you the lowdown on spell work. It's a potent tool that witches use to manifest their desires and make changes in the world around them. But don't get it twisted, we're not talking about waving a wand and turning a pumpkin into a carriage. This is serious business, folks.

Spellwork is all about harnessing the energy and channelling it towards a specific goal. Witches use various tools like candles, herbs, crystals, and sigils to focus their energy and amplify their intentions. It's like giving the universe a little push in the right direction.

Don't let the fear of creating your first spell hold you back. You don't need a fancy cauldron or expensive crystals to get started. All you need is your magical intention and a little creativity.

That's right, any object can become charged with energy, so don't be afraid to use what you have on hand. Raid your spice cabinet and grab some, cinnamon, black pepper, or cayenne pepper. These bad boys are powerful spices that can be used in oils, potions, and infusions to work some serious magic.

And don't forget about your cooking pots . They can become your cauldrons in a snap! Just be sure to give them a good scrub before using them for magical purposes. As for candles, almost any candle can be transformed into a magical tool, but let's be real, that "Bahama Breeze" Yankee Candle may not be the best choice for your spellwork. But hey, if that's all you've got, it's better than nothing, right?

So go ahead, let your creative juices flow and create some magical goodness. And remember, your intention is the most important ingredient of all. So put some love and positive energy into your spells, and watch the magic unfold.

But here's the kicker: spellwork isn't just about getting what you want. It's about aligning your energy with the energy of the universe and working together to create positive change. It's about tapping into your intuition and connection to the divine to build a better world for yourself and those around you.

The key to success is all about starting with purpose. You can't just throw together a bunch of ingredients and hope for the best. Your spell needs to come from a deep desire or need within you. Maybe it's a response to a recent opportunity, or maybe it's a newfound interest in the magickal arts, but it needs to come from a place of intention.

Now, listen up, because this is important: crafting a spell while in the throes of extreme emotional stress is a no-go. If you're fueled by frenzy, you can expect erratic results. So, take a deep breath and get centred before you start. Channel your magickal energy with focus, wisdom, and empathy. Your outcome will always reflect your temperament at the time of creation.

Remember, when you're creating a spell, you're tapping into the power of the universe. That's some serious stuff, so don't take it lightly. Your intentions should be pure, and your heart should be open. When you put that kind of energy out into the world, it will come back to you tenfold. So, take your time, set your intention, and let the magick flow. The universe is waiting to work with you.

There are different types of spell work. First up, we've got candle magic. This is all about using coloured candles to focus your energy and intention towards a specific goal. Want to attract love or money? There's a candle for that.

Next up, we've got herb magic. This is all about using herbs and plants to create potions and incense that can help you manifest your desires. Whether you're looking for protection, healing, or prosperity, there's a herb out there that can do the trick.

Then there's crystal magic. Crystals are like little energy batteries. They can be used to amplify your intentions and connect you to the energy of the universe. Whether you're using them for meditation, healing, or manifestation, crystals are a powerful tool for any witch.

Sigil magic is another form of spell work that involves creating symbols or designs to represent your desires. Once you've created your sigil, you can charge it with your energy and use it to manifest your intention. It's like creating your own personal logo.

Last but not least, we've got moon magic. This is all about harnessing the energy of the moon to help you manifest your desires. Whether you're doing a full moon ritual to release what no longer serves you or a new moon ritual to set new intentions, working with the phases of the moon can be a powerful way to amplify your magic.

But when it comes to spell work, there's no one-size-fits-all solution. Some witches stick to the tried-and-true methods passed down through generations, while others prefer to trust their gut and let their intuition guide them. As for me, I fall into the latter category. I don't believe in limiting myself to one particular style of witchcraft - I let my creativity flow and write my own spells, casting incantations that come straight from the heart.

As a child, I never realised that my knack for writing poetry and songs was actually a form of spell work. But looking back, it all makes sense now. And I'm not afraid to share my unique creations with the world, . Whether it's through my social media channels or in-person gatherings, I love spreading the word about the power of magic and how it can transform your life. So if you're feeling stuck or in need of a little extra juju, don't be afraid to tap into your own creative energy and write your own spells. Trust me, the results can be truly magical.

So if you're curious about spell work, dive in and explore. But remember, with great power comes great responsibility. Be mindful of your intentions and the impact they might have on others. And if you need guidance, there are plenty of resources out there to help you on your path.

If you're looking to expand your knowledge on witchcraft and spell work, then I've got some spicy recommendations for you. Let's start with the queen of modern witchcraft, the one and only, Lisa Lister. Her book, "Witch: Unleashed. Untamed. Unapologetic." is a must-read for anyone looking to embrace their inner witch and connect with their feminine power.

Next up, we've got "The Modern Witchcraft Spell Book" by Skye Alexander. This book is chock-full of spells for all occasions, from love and money to protection and healing. It's a great resource for beginner and advanced witches alike.

If you're looking for a historical perspective on witchcraft, then check out "Witches, Sluts, Feminists: Conjuring the Sex Positive" by Kristen J. Sollee. This book explores the intersection of witchcraft, feminism, and sexuality throughout history and offers a fresh perspective on what it means to be a witch in modern times.

And let's not forget "The Green Witch: Your Complete Guide to the Natural Magic of Herbs, Flowers, Essential Oils, and More" by Arin Murphy-Hiscock. This book is all about using natural ingredients to create powerful spells and connect with the earth. It's perfect for anyone looking to deepen their connection with nature and incorporate more green witchcraft into their practice.

CHAPTER 10: DIMENSIONS, ETS AND STAR SEEDS, OH MY!

In this chapter, we're gonna go galactic. This is what I mean about when my life became Star Wars. Even writing about this, I feel so out there, and I know some people be reading this and thinking what the hell is she talking about? But I can promise you that it is all entirely real.

There's so much more to this universe and will ever know, I'm really only on the precipice of even discovering ourselves, and the tiny amounts that we know about our earth and our brain. And really the full power of all potential. And on that premise there are so many more lifeforms out there, so much more to the universe, the Multiverse and everything in between. There's a real link between quantum physics and spirituality, and I've always had such an interest in both and I never knew why before. It's only in recent times that I started to see the correlation between it.

LET'S TALK DIMENSIONS:

Dimensions are like different levels of existence, each with its own set of rules and energy vibes. As you move up the ladder, you gain a higher perspective and more power to manifest your reality.

When it comes to spirituality, dimensions are like levels of consciousness, perception, and awareness. But don't get it twisted, we're not talking about physical places you can measure with a ruler. Nope, these dimensions are all about how you feel and experience the world around you.

Think of it like this - you're on a journey inward, and these dimensions are like signposts that help you know where you're at in your consciousness. It's like having a map to guide you on your climb to the top. Sure, you might pass through different dimensions along the way, but you're only conscious of them when you focus your awareness on them.

And listen up, these dimensions ain't the same as the dimensions of space, okay? So don't go thinking that just because you're on a higher level of consciousness, you're floating off into another dimension. Nope, most of these dimensions exist right here in our reality of three-dimensional space and beyond. So keep your feet on the ground, , and keep climbing those dimensions!

The first two dimensions are all about physical existence - what's inside and what's outside of things. But the third dimension, well that's where us humans come in. That's our normal level of consciousness, made up of our thoughts and emotions about our own lives and the lives of others.

Now, let me tell you something - there are levels to this sh*t. That's right, there are different dimensions of consciousness that we can operate on, ranging from basic instincts to super-elevated states. And let me tell you, , the level you're on can make all the difference in how you experience life.

Feeling stuck in a routine or lacking inspiration? You might be operating on a low-dimensional level, my friend. But if you're feeling a sense of purpose and connection to the world around you, well then you might just be on a higher-dimensional level.

But here's the tea - these dimensions aren't something you can measure or touch. They're all about your own personal experience and perception. So if you want to live your best life, you better start leveling up that consciousness and tapping into those positive emotions like love, joy, and peace. Get ready to feel that heightened awareness, , and start living your best life in all dimensions.

I love Dr David R. Hawkins's teachings on human consciousness and its associated energy fields. I learned about this through my kinesiology sessions, where my practitioner would measure where my energy field was in terms of levels of consciousness. Finally, someone's providing a roadmap for the stages of enlightenment! It's about time we have a concrete way to measure our personal vibration and figure out where we stand on the scale of evolution. This info is gold and can be applied in so many ways, I can't even begin to count.

It's like an energetic frequency that we emit and can be measured on The Map of Consciousness. Dr. David R. Hawkins spent 20 years researching and calibrating different attitudes and emotions to define these levels. He wrote about it in his book *Power vs. Force* and it's super interesting!

By using a muscle-testing method, he assigned a log number to each level based on its energy response to a stimulus. The scale ranges from Shame, Guilt, and Anger to Love, Peace, and Enlightenment. And the best part is that there are visual charts and practical applications for healing and recovery in *The Map of Consciousness Explained.*

So if you want to learn more about the different levels of consciousness and how you can use them to improve your life, definitely check out this book!

Moving up the consciousness scale is a gradual process of learning how to respond to events in the world with better thoughts. Once you start climbing that ladder, life gets real juicy. You start feeling more fulfilled and connected to others, and you finally figure out your own purpose and values. It's not always gonna be rainbows and unicorns, but the payoff is totally worth it.

The map looks something like this:

Enlightenment 700 – 1,000

Starting at the tippy-top of the list is enlightenment, only achieved by the ascended masters like Buddha and Jesus. And just thinking about those dudes can lift you up, so they're basically consciousness boosters.

Peace 600 – 700

If you're not quite there yet, you can try reaching the level of peace, which is all about stealing your mind.

Joy 540 – 600

Or if you're feeling joyful, you might be on the level of advanced spiritual people, releasing your personal story and ego in order to get in tune with harmony.

Love 500- 540

Then there's the level of love, which is all about selflessness and doing good without expecting anything in return. This is using your logic in service of the higher good.

Reason 400 – 500

This level of consciousness is all about upgrading yourself and ditching the things that no longer work for you. But hold up, there's a catch! It's easy to get so obsessed with learning that you forget about the real juicy bits that matter. Don't get so caught up in studying that you miss the whole point .

Acceptance 350 – 400

Say goodbye to that victim mentality and hello to being in charge of your own destiny. It's time to set those goals and start working towards them like the creator you are.

Willingness 310 – 350

You've reached the level of optimism where you see challenges as opportunities and start forming some sweet self-discipline.

NEUTRALITY
250 – 310

At this level, you may feel like you're coasting without any real direction or ambition, but hey, at least you're content with where you're at.

COURAGE 200 – 250

At this level, you're no longer a slave to your emotions, but rather, you take charge of your life by responding to situations instead of reacting to them. It's like putting on your superhero cape and feeling totally empowered.

PRIDE 175 – 200

At this point, you're feeling more positive than the below states, but still attached to the external world.

ANGER 150 – 175

At the lower levels of consciousness, you may find yourself stuck in a vicious cycle of external circumstances leading to anger. But hey, it can also be the catalyst for change, or the beginning of a long and frustrating plateau.

DESIRE 125 – 150

At this level, you can be consumed by an insatiable appetite for power, money, sex, and status, leading to an unhealthy attachment to external goals

FEAR 100 – 125

At this level, the world seems like a constant enemy, and paranoia runs high.

GRIEF 75 – 100

It can be difficult to navigate life at this level of consciousness, as you may struggle with processing their emotions and constantly feel like they are falling short. It's important to approach oneself with compassion and understanding during this time and to seek support and resources to help with emotional processing and personal growth.

APATHY 50 – 75

At this level, you may experience a sense of hopelessness and numbness, and like you might have no control over your circumstances. You may see yourself as a victim of your situation, struggling to find a way out. It can be a challenging and difficult place to be in, and it's important to approach it with empathy and understanding.

GUILT 30 – 50

At this level, you may dislike your own actions rather than yourself, leading to an inability to forgive yourself and feelings of worthlessness.

SHAME BELOW 30

This level is marked by a deep sense of feeling flawed at the very core of one's being. Shame and thoughts of self-harm may arise in this state.

If you're still stuck in the lower levels, like being all about desire and attachment to external goals, then you can get help to heal and move up.

Going to kinesiology was a game changer for me in terms of moving out of the lower levels of consciousness and healing my trauma. Through the removal of negative energy, I was able to operate at higher levels of consciousness, reaching level 500 from my initial starting point of level 100.

It's important to note that these levels can fluctuate throughout our journeys, but the progress I made through kinesiology helped me to feel better and experience a greater sense of inner peace. Overall, it was a powerful tool in my healing process and personal growth.

If you're feeling guilty about your current state of consciousness, don't worry. That's just a level too. Shame is the bottom of the barrel, with feelings of worthlessness and suicidal thoughts.

If you wanna dive deeper into this whole consciousness topic, you can check out Power vs. Force by David Hawkins.

STARSEEDS:

You may have heard a lot of people talking about Starseeds. They're all over the Internet, TikTok and the 'gram. Starseeds are advanced souls from other planets and realms who possess spiritual and scientific knowledge that dates back hundreds of thousands of years. Yeah, you heard me right - these folks are out-of-this-world smart! And get this, they're here on Earth to inspire and heal us, mere mortals. They bring light and knowledge to uplift the human race and awaken our consciousness to help the planet evolve. But here's the kicker - when they get here, they forget all about their true origins and missions. Talk about a bummer, right? But don't worry, once they awaken, they remember their purpose and get to work living it out. So, if you ever meet a Starseed, be sure to thank them for all the inspiration and healing they're bringing to the planet.

A lot of these folks have been awake since a young age. Once you've seen the light, you can't go back to meaningless conversations, jobs, and relationships. These folks know they're here for a reason and they get really frustrated with how slow everyone else is to catch up. And you know what else? They feel like they just don't fit in with the rest of us mere mortals. They remember some other place, but they can't quite put their finger on it, and it's like they're constantly searching for a way to feel more 'at home.' I mean, can you blame them? Being a Starseed can't be easy when you're lightyears ahead of everyone else.

So apparently, some of these folks feel so different that they spend a good chunk of their lives trying to fit into some sort of box or hiding their true selves. But let me tell you, that goes against everything they stand for as spiritual beings! The more they try to hide, the more alone and unseen they feel. But when they embrace their uniqueness and show the world who they truly are, they create a life that's in alignment with their soul's purpose. It's like they say, "you do you, boo," and your people will find you. And don't even get me started on why we incarnate on Earth - apparently, it's all about experiencing life in a human body and growing our souls.

If you're asking how to tell if you're a Starseed, then you probably already are one. But just to be sure, here are five ways to know for sure:

1. You feel like you don't belong here: If you've always felt like you don't quite fit in on this planet, then you might be a Starseed. Maybe you find human society to be too shallow or materialistic, or perhaps you have a longing for something deeper and more meaningful. Either way, your soul might be longing for the cosmic home that you left behind.

2. You have a deep spiritual yearning: Starseeds tend to have a natural affinity for all things spiritual. Maybe you're drawn to astrology, meditation, or energy healing. Or perhaps you have a strong connection to nature or a deep appreciation for the beauty of the cosmos. Whatever it is, your soul is searching for a connection to something greater than yourself.

3. You're highly empathic: Starseeds tend to be highly sensitive to the emotions and energies of others. You might find that you easily pick up on other people's moods, or that you feel drained after spending time in large crowds. This is because your soul is attuned to the subtle energies of the universe.

4. You have a strong sense of purpose: Starseeds often feel a strong sense of mission or purpose in life. You

might have a deep desire to help others or to make a difference in the world. This is because your soul remembers the important work that you came here to do.

5. You have a fascination with the stars: Starseeds often have a deep love and fascination for the stars and the cosmos. You might feel drawn to astronomy or have a special affinity for a particular star or constellation. This is because your soul remembers the beauty and wonder of the universe from which you came.

So there you have it, my cosmic cutie. If these five signs resonate with you, then you're probably a Starseed. Embrace your cosmic heritage. But, with so many different types of Starseeds out there, it can definitely feel overwhelming trying to figure out which one you are. But remember, at the end of the day, your Starseed heritage is just one small piece of your cosmic puzzle. You are a unique and beautiful soul, and your journey is your own. Don't get too caught up in trying to fit into a specific category or label. Instead, focus on exploring your own inner world and discovering your own unique gifts and talents. And who knows, maybe you'll discover that you have a little bit of every Starseed energy within you. At the end of the day , what matters most is that you shine bright like the star that you are, no matter which star system you come from.

The different types of Starseeds:

There are more types of Starseeds than there are shades of lipstick! But don't worry, I'll break it down for you in my signature sassy style.

1. Pleiadian Starseeds: These Starseeds come from the Pleiades star system and are known for their gentle, nurturing energy. They are often empathic, intuitive, and creative, with a strong desire to help others. Think of them as the cosmic equivalent of a warm hug.

2. Sirius Starseeds: Sirius Starseeds come from the Sirius star system and are known for their wisdom and intelligence. They are often natural leaders, with a strong sense of purpose and a desire to create positive change in the world. Think of them as the cosmic equivalent of a boss babe.

3. Arcturian Starseeds: Arcturian Starseeds come from the Arcturus star system and are known for their advanced spiritual knowledge and healing abilities. They are often highly empathic and have a strong connection to nature. Think of them as the cosmic equivalent of a witchy healer.

4. Andromedan Starseeds: Andromedan Starseeds come from the Andromeda galaxy and are known for their strength, courage, and determination. They are often warriors for peace, with a strong desire to protect the earth and its inhabitants. Think of them as the cosmic equivalent of a fierce warrior princess.

5. Pleiadian-Sirian Hybrid Starseeds: These Starseeds are a mix of Pleiadian and Sirius energy, and are known for their balance of intuition and intelligence. They are often highly creative and have a deep love for music and the arts. Think of them as the cosmic equivalent of a multi-talented superstar.

6. Lyran Starseeds: Lyran Starseeds Come from the Lyra constellation and are known for their high energy and strong willpower. They are often passionate and driven, with a deep desire to explore the mysteries of the universe. Think of them as the cosmic equivalent of a fiery entrepreneur.

These are just a few examples of the different types of Starseeds Out there. One of the beauties of being a cosmic soul is that you have had multiple lives across different star systems. That's right, you might have been a Pleiadian in one lifetime, and a Lyran in another. It's like being a chameleon, but on a cosmic scale! But no matter which star system you come from, you're here on earth for a reason.

I used to feel so lonely and out of place on this Earth. I mean, don't get me wrong, I love it here, but there was always this nagging feeling in the back of my mind that I didn't quite belong.

I used to dream about going to space, exploring the cosmos and finding a place where I truly fit in. But then I started exploring my Starseed heritage, and everything changed.

I learned about my origins, about where I come from and what makes me unique. And let me tell you, it was like a weight had been lifted off my shoulders.

Suddenly, I didn't feel so alone anymore. I knew that there were others out there who shared my heritage and my experiences, and that gave me a sense of belonging that I had never felt before.

So if you're feeling lost and alone, my dear, I encourage you to explore your Starseed heritage. Dive into the knowledge and wisdom that's out there, and start learning about who you truly are.

Because once you know where you come from, everything else falls into place. You start to see the world with new eyes, and you realise that you are part of something much bigger than yourself.

Finding out which Starseed you are is like finding the perfect shade of lipstick - it takes some experimentation and a little bit of trial and error. But don't worry, I'll give you some tips on how to figure it out.

1. Look to the stars: One of the easiest ways to figure out which Starseed you are is to look to the stars. Maybe you feel a deep connection to a particular star or constellation. Do some research on the different star

systems and see which ones resonate with you.

2. Pay attention to your strengths: Another clue to your Starseed heritage is to pay attention to your strengths and natural abilities. Are you highly empathic and intuitive like a Pleiadian? Or are you a natural leader with a strong sense of purpose like a Sirius Starseed? Your innate talents can give you a clue to your cosmic origins.

3. Listen to your intuition: Your intuition is your inner guidance system, and it can be a powerful tool in helping you discover your Starseed heritage. Trust your gut and listen to your inner voice. It may lead you to the answers you're seeking.

4. Explore different modalities: There are many different modalities out there that can help you discover your Starseed heritage, such as meditation, hypnosis, and past life regression. Explore different options and see what resonates with you.

5. Embrace your uniqueness: At the end of the day, , you are a unique and beautiful soul, and your Starseed heritage is just one aspect of your cosmic makeup. Embrace your individuality and don't worry too much about fitting into a specific box. After all, who wants to be just like everyone else anyway?

You can meditate on which Starseed you are too. Follow this exercise:

First, find a quiet and comfortable place where you won't be disturbed. Light a few candles, burn some incense, and get your favorite crystals out, because we're going to get all kinds of woo-woo up in here.

Next, close your eyes and take a few deep breaths, inhaling all that cosmic energy and exhaling any stress or worries you may be carrying.

Now, visualise yourself standing in front of a door. This

door represents your cosmic origins, and behind it lies the knowledge of which Starseed you truly are.

As you reach for the doorknob, feel the excitement and anticipation building within you. This is your moment!

As you swing the door open, allow yourself to be bathed in a bright and beautiful light. This light represents the energy of your Starseed heritage.

Now, ask the universe to reveal to you which Starseed energy you possess. Allow yourself to receive any images, sounds, or sensations that come to you. Don't try to force anything, just allow the knowledge to flow to you naturally.

Take as long as you need to connect with this energy and truly understand it. When you feel ready, take a deep breath and thank the universe for this beautiful gift of knowledge.

So there you have it, my cosmic cutie. Use these tips as a starting point to discovering your Starseed heritage, but remember to trust your intuition and embrace your own unique journey. And who knows, maybe you're a hybrid Starseed, combining the best qualities of multiple star systems. Now that's something to sashay and slay about!

On multiple lives:

Let's talk about coming to Earth as a Starseed. You see, as a cosmic soul, you've had multiple lives across different star systems. But you didn't just come to Earth for the scenery, you came here with a mission.

You see, Earth is in a bit of a sticky situation right now. She's been through the wringer, and she needs all the help she can get.

We've got things like greed, hate, and fear that can drag us and this planet down faster than a lead balloon. We've got pollution, deforestation, and other forms of environmental destruction that can wreak havoc on the planet's delicate ecosystem.

But don't worry, because there's hope. You see, as humans, we also have the power to raise the vibration of this planet.

We can choose to be kind, compassionate, and empathetic towards others. We can choose to protect and preserve the environment instead of exploiting and destroying it. We can choose to focus on the positive instead of dwelling on the negative.

And don't forget, we're not alone in this. There are other humans and Starseeds out there who are working towards the same goal. So let's team up and spread those good vibes far and wide.

That's where you come in. You came to Earth with a purpose - to help raise the vibration and bring more love, light, and positivity to this planet.

Healing yourself and living in alignment is a key aspect of how you can raise the vibration of this planet as a Starseed.

Taking care of yourself is not only beneficial for you, but it also benefits the planet. When you're in a good place, mentally, emotionally, and spiritually, you emit positive energy out into the world.

This energy can inspire others to care for themselves and make positive changes in their lives, creating a ripple effect that spreads far and wide, ultimately raising the vibration of this planet one person at a time.

Living in alignment with your true self is also crucial, as it enables you to tap into a higher power, cosmic energy that can aid you in bringing positive change to the world.

Therefore, prioritize your mental, emotional, and spiritual well-being. Seek out healing modalities that resonate with you, whether that's meditation, yoga, therapy, or another form of healing.

Remember that by healing yourself, you're also contributing to the healing of the planet. So, let's work together to raise the vibration of this planet one healed soul at a time.

I know it can be tempting to put others' needs before your own, especially when you're working towards such an important goal. But let me tell you, you can't pour from an empty cup.

I used to put everyone else before myself. I thought that if I could be there for everyone with the best advice on solving their problems, it would make me lovable and needed. I never thought I was good enough just by myself, so I overdid it, and I burned out.

It took me a while to realise that putting everyone else before myself was actually doing more harm than good. I was constantly exhausted and stressed, and I was neglecting my own needs in the process.

But eventually, I hit a breaking point. I realised that I couldn't continue to pour from an empty cup. I needed to prioritize myself and my own well-being.

But it wasn't until I started doing some inner work that I realised where that behaviour was coming from. It was a trauma response to a deep-seated belief that I wasn't good enough just as I was.

And let me tell you, it's especially pervasive for women. We're often socialised to believe that our worth is tied to our ability to care for others, so we can fall into the trap of putting everyone else first.

And let me tell you, it was one of the best decisions I ever made. I started setting boundaries and taking time for myself, and it made all the difference.

I realised that I didn't have to be everything to everyone to be lovable or needed. I am worthy and valuable just as I am, and I don't need to overdo it to prove my worth.

Taking care of yourself and setting boundaries is key to being an effective Starseeds. It allows you to be fully present and grounded, ready to take on the challenges that come with raising the vibration of this planet.

So don't be afraid to say no when you need to. Don't be afraid to take a break and recharge your batteries. Remember, you're not being selfish, you're being smart.

So if you find yourself constantly putting others first, take a step back and ask yourself where that's coming from. Is it a trauma response? A belief that you're not good enough?

And by taking care of yourself, you're also setting an example for others. You're showing them that it's okay to prioritize their own needs and that doing so can actually help them be more effective in their own mission.

So, take care of yourself. Set those boundaries. And remember, you're not just doing it for you, you're doing it for the planet.

Feeling lonely as a Starseed is a common experience. We come from different planets and galaxies, and it can feel like we don't quite fit in here on Earth.

And sometimes, we try to fill that void by being there for everyone else. But let me tell you, that's not the solution.

You see, the only way to truly connect with others is by first connecting with yourself. And as a Starseed, that means connecting with your heritage.

It's only when we understand who we are and where we come from that we can truly feel grounded and whole. And from that place of wholeness, we can start to form deep and meaningful connections with others.

So if you're feeling lonely and isolated, my dear, take a step back and start connecting with yourself. Dive into your Starseed heritage and start exploring who you truly are. Because it's only by filling up that hole within yourself that you can truly connect with others in a deep and meaningful way.

And trust me, once you start connecting with your true self and your Starseed heritage, you'll find that you're never truly alone. The universe is vast and full of possibilities, and there's always someone or something out there that resonates with who you are at your core.

Now, I know it can be tough out there. You might feel like you don't fit in or like you're not from here. But , that's because you're not! You're a Starseed on a mission, and that mission is to help heal this planet and its people.

So don't be afraid to embrace your cosmic heritage, my dear. Use your cosmic knowledge and experience to help bring positive change to the world around you. Whether it's through art, music, activism, or simply being a shining example of love and kindness, every little bit counts.

And remember , you're not alone. There are other Starseeds out there, just like you, who are working towards the same goal.

If you're feeling like you don't belong on this planet, it's gonna hold you back from reaching your full potential. Those fears and doubts can be some powerful blocks, but you gotta work through 'em if you wanna advance. I know it can be tough out here, but giving up and wanting to bounce is not the solution.

If you're truly serious about wanting to go back to your cosmic crib, then you need to start understanding and working with those feelings. You can't just ignore 'em and hope they go away. That's not gonna get you anywhere except stuck in the same place. And , that's not gonna help you fulfill your contract.

So it's time to roll up your sleeves and get to work. Face those fears, deal with those doubts, and get on with the business of living. 'Cause trust me, there's a whole lotta good you can do here on Earth if you're willing to put in the effort.

So keep shining your cosmic light, my dear, and let's make this world a better place, one sassy step at a time!

CONNECTING WITH ETS:

There's a whole bunch of galactic beings out there who are watching over us like proud parents at a talent show. They're rooting for us to raise our vibration and evolve into the best versions of ourselves.

And let's be real, who wouldn't want to be part of that squad? These aliens have got some serious knowledge and wisdom, and they're more than happy to share it with us. They know that we're capable of amazing things, and they're here to help us unlock our full potential.

But it's not all one-sided, you know. We've got a job to do too. Part of our mission as Starseeds is to awaken to our true selves, to remember who we are and where we come from. And that's why it's called a spiritual awakening .

It's not always easy, I'll give you that. Sometimes it feels like we're stumbling around in the dark, trying to find our way. But that's where those alien guides come in. They're like the light at the end of the tunnel, showing us the way forward.

My first connection was something that I really wasn't expecting. I've never really done the whole psychedelics or plant medicine thing, but on one such occasion a few years ago there was a global meditation happening. And I connected with a few of my friends who were further down the spiritual path than I was, and we were part of a whole group of people around the world that were tuning into this global meditation online

Anyway, so we're tuning in and we'd had some psychedelics to help the experience, and we made a crystal grid to protect our energy from any lower dimensional beings. And the whole idea was as this person on the video was holding the meditation we meditated with him, and we were going to heal the earth because he was part of the pandemic. And as that started happening and we were envisioning being in space and holding our hands to heal the earth, I looked to my right and saw a FREAKING SPACESHIP. I was looking around space, where I could see no one else and I was like is anybody else doing this? And anyway I thought well I've always wanted to see a spaceship so I might as well go and visit inside, and as I did they were these amazing eight or nine-foot beings who are blue and had no hair, we're very slender and look to be wearing medieval garbs. They had a very nice nature and energy about them and were smiling at my wonder of their spaceship. Anyways I felt like when I spoke to them they understood me, but I couldn't understand them and now I understand because they were talking telepathically and I just didn't have the right sense of consciousness to understand. But they smiled all the way. And I asked for a tour of the spaceship, which they absolutely love so I got to float through it all, and then when I opened my eyes and explained this to my friends, they said that I'd had encounters with higher dimensional beings.

Not all aliens are hanging out in our plain old dimension, okay? Some of these extraterrestrial beings are so advanced that they don't need to physically exist to be seen. They're playing the game on a whole 'nother level, in an interdimensional realm. Tapping into plant medicine can help expand your consciousness and connect you with these next-level entities.

For the next few days, I thought about this really interesting encounter that I'd have. It felt really real, and I've learnt to trust my feelings that if something feels really real, then it means it is real. Even if I didn't have the words or experience or really the people to talk to about it. So I did what any person does when a new experience happens, I googled the shit out of it. And what I found was lots of other experiences with other people who had also met these beings. And I described perfectly what I saw, in the same way that I described above. To my huge surprise, lots of other people had encountered them. And the name for this race of beings was the Arcturians.

After my mind-bending journey with plant medicine, I was determined to learn more about these blue-skinned Arcturian beings who took me to space. I dove headfirst into podcasts and books to understand their culture, customs, and ways of operation. The more I learned, the more I realised that the Arcturians have been silently guiding humanity for centuries. Their tall, slender bodies and almond-shaped eyes are just the tip of the iceberg. They have been working with us to raise the vibration of the planet and make it a better place. Educating myself on their ways has truly been a life-changing experience, and I am grateful for their guidance.

The Arcturians have a humanoid appearance with blue skin and large, almond-shaped eyes. They are also described as tall and slender, with elongated fingers and limbs. The Arcturians can shape-shift or project their consciousness in different forms, depending on the situation or the individual they are interacting with. So I found it really interesting that they projected themselves and exactly how they were, because I must've been at a level of consciousness with the plant medicine in order to not be scared by that.

I started reading some amazing books, where the author was channelling Arcturians and the way they work with the earth. It felt so right to me. So true. I learnt so much about them. This set of books is called "Connecting with the Arcturians" by David K Miller and I HIGHLY recommend them. There may also be books out there, with people channelling the Starseeds that you come from and you can look for those books and find out more about them that way as well.

These celestial beings are not your average run-of-the-mill extraterrestrials. They are fifth-dimensional beings, which means they operate on a higher frequency than us mere mortals. Their consciousness transcends time and space, allowing them to see the bigger picture and operate with a level of wisdom and love that we can only dream of. They are all about healing and raising the vibration of the planet, which is why they often work with Starseeds like us. So if you want to hang with the Arcturians, you better start practicing your meditation and raising your own vibration , because they operate on a whole other level.

These fifth-dimensional beings don't just work alone, oh no. They team up with the angels and ascended masters to help raise the vibration of the planet. It's like a cosmic Avengers team, but instead of battling evil, they're battling negative energy and low vibrations. The Arcturians bring their wisdom and healing abilities, the angels bring their divine guidance and protection, and the ascended masters bring their experience and enlightenment. Together, they form a powerhouse team that is dedicated to helping us all reach a higher level of consciousness.

Working with galactic beings can be a game-changer for your consciousness. It's like getting a VIP pass to the cosmic club, where you can learn and grow beyond the limitations of this three-dimensional world. When you connect with these higher dimensional beings, they can help expand your understanding of the universe and your place in it. And the best part? They don't have any of the ego or baggage that us humans tend to carry around.

I've now started connecting to the Arcturians, without needing plant medicine a little and have used my psychic medium gifts in order to channel messages from them, both by automatic writing and also just by speaking telepathically to them. Both of which sounded absolutely mental to me until I started doing them. How I know I am not speaking to myself, is because the words that they use would never be ones that I would EVER think of.. Especially when I was reading them back.

The way that we communicate, comes out as English and the way that I write it. But there's also an intergalactic language that many beings use called Light Language. Light language is a divine form of communication that channels cosmic energy and sound to deliver messages that are interpreted by the heart and resonate with the soul, rather than relying on the limitations of programmed hearing and the brain. Light language is the ultimate power move when it comes to expressing energies that go beyond what our boring human languages can handle. Your soul is too magnificent to be contained by mere words, just like the vastness of the universe can't be expressed in a single sentence. By tapping into Light Language, you're unleashing a tsunami of energy, light, and power that's just waiting to be expressed in your life. You can listen to a lot of white language healings on TikTok and YouTube, and there are also meditation so that you can start to use it and even start using it yourself. Sometimes you just need to be exposed to something first in order to understand it, get a grasp and then people to do it yourself. And it actually will go to the part of your body that needs it the most. Because it's so advanced it's more like a feeling rather than understanding it with the mind.

And so when I'm communicating, I use less of this and more of my own language because these beings are so advanced that they can automatically just speak the language that you use, and the same way that they can shapeshift to a way that is most comfortable for you to experience at the level that you're at.

When we undergo a spiritual awakening, we're not only waking up to our own truth and purpose, but we're also awakening to the interconnectedness of all things. We begin to recognize that we're not separate from the world around us, but rather, we're part of a larger whole.

As we awaken to this truth, we start to see that the world is in need of healing and transformation. We realize that we're living in a world that operates from a low vibration of fear, lack, and scarcity, and that this is creating immense suffering for ourselves and for the planet as a whole.

To bring about change and shift to a higher dimension, we need to focus on our own healing and growth first. This is because we're all connected energetically, and our individual vibration affects the collective vibration.

As we heal and raise our own vibration, we contribute to the healing and transformation of the collective consciousness. We become a beacon of light and inspiration for others to follow, and we help to create a ripple effect of positive change.

But spiritual awakening is just the beginning of the journey. It's a lifelong process of growth, learning, and evolution. It's important to remember that it's not a destination, but a continual unfolding.

As we continue down the path of spiritual growth, we begin to understand that there are many dimensions of reality beyond the physical realm. We start to tap into higher realms of consciousness and expand our understanding of the universe.

By operating from a higher vibration of love, joy, and gratitude, we can help to bring about a shift in the collective consciousness. We can create a world that operates from a higher vibration, where love, peace, and harmony are the norm.

But to do this, we need to be willing to do the inner work, to heal our own wounds, and to align our thoughts, feelings, and beliefs with what we want to manifest. We need to show up authentically, live our truth, and be a positive force for change in the world.

In this way, we can help to bring about the shift to a new dimension and create a world that operates from a higher vibration.

Through my experiences with plant medicine and connecting with galactic beings, I began to understand that there is so much more to this universe than what we can see with our physical senses. It was through these experiences that I realized that my connection to these higher dimensions was not just my imagination, but a real and tangible experience.

Through plant medicine, I was able to connect with higher realms of consciousness and gain a deeper understanding of the universe. I was able to see that we're not alone in this world, and that there are beings from other dimensions who are here to support us on our journey.

It was through these connections that I began to understand the importance of healing as a collective. We're all connected energetically, and our individual healing contributes to the healing of the collective. When we heal ourselves, we create a ripple effect of positive change that extends far beyond our own individual experience.

This is where angels come in. Angels are beings of light who exist in higher dimensions and are here to support us on our journey. They can help us to connect with our inner wisdom, find our purpose, and heal our wounds.

Through my experiences with plant medicine and connecting with galactic beings, I began to see that angels are just one of the many beings who are here to support us. There are also spirit guides, ascended masters, and other entities who are here to help us on our journey.

The important thing is to remain open and receptive to these higher realms of consciousness, and to cultivate a deep sense of trust in our own intuition and inner wisdom. When we do this, we can tap into the infinite wisdom of the universe and connect with the beings who are here to support us on our journey.

In this way, we can heal ourselves and contribute to the healing of the collective. We can create a world that operates from a higher vibration of love and light, where we're all connected and supported on our journey.

CHAPTER 11: GET YOUR CRYSTAL ON

This chapter is like a love letter to one of my absolute faves: the sparkly, the enchanting, the downright gorgeous. I'm talking about crystals. These babies are so special to me, I could just gush about them for days. We're diving deep into their properties and how they can help you on your spiritual journey, so get ready to feel some seriously good vibes. Let's get to work, crystal queens and kings!

Crystals are like little energy powerhouses, and they work their magic by vibrating at specific frequencies that can affect our own energy fields. See, every crystal has a unique molecular structure and composition, which gives it its own special properties and abilities.

When you work with crystals in spirituality, you're essentially tapping into their energy and using it to enhance your own. Whether you're looking to attract love, manifest abundance, or connect with your higher self, there's a crystal out there that can help.

Some folks like to meditate with crystals, holding them in their hand or placing them on different parts of their body to help balance and align their energy centres. Others like to wear them as jewellery, so they can carry the crystal's energy with them throughout the day. And some even like to grid their homes or workspaces with different crystals, creating a harmonious and high-vibe environment.

We're gonna dive into the seven most popular ones and all their juicy properties. Get ready to take some notes, because these babies are gonna change your life!

First up, we have Amethyst:

Amethyst is like a spa day for your mind. This gorgeous purple crystal is the ultimate stress-buster, and it'll have you feeling zen in no time. Feeling frazzled after a long day? Just pop an Amethyst under your pillow, and let the magic happen. You'll be snoozing like a baby and waking up feeling like a million bucks.

But that's not all, darlin'. Amethyst is also a powerhouse for spiritual growth and intuition. It'll help you tap into your inner wisdom and connect with your higher self. And if you're someone who struggles with anxiety or negative thought patterns, Amethyst is the perfect crystal for you. It'll soothe your nerves and help you stay grounded, even in the midst of chaos.

So if you're looking for a little bit of calm in your life, don't sleep on Amethyst. This purple beauty is like a big ol' hug from the universe, and it'll have you feeling peaceful, centreed, and ready to take on whatever comes your way. Trust me, , once you try Amethyst, you'll wonder how you ever lived without it.

Next, we have Rose Quartz, the stone of love:

Rose Quartz is the ultimate love magnet. This pink powerhouse is like a big ol' hug from the universe, and it'll have you feeling all warm and fuzzy inside. Whether you're looking for a romantic partner or just want to deepen your connections with the people you love, Rose Quartz is the crystal for you.

Just hold it close to your heart, and let the love flow, baby. Rose Quartz will help you open up your heart chakra and attract all kinds of love and affection into your life. It's like a little love potion, but without all the creepy magic stuff. And if you're someone who struggles with self-love and self-care, Rose Quartz will help you see yourself through the eyes of love and compassion.

So if you're ready to up your love game, don't sleep on Rose Quartz. This pink beauty is like a big ol' dose of heart-opening magic, and it'll have you feeling loved, appreciated, and supported in no time. Trust me, once you try Rose Quartz, you'll wonder how you ever lived without it.

Third on the list is Citrine, the stone of abundance:

Citrine is like a little bag of money magic. This yellow beauty is the ultimate stone of abundance, and it'll have you manifesting success and wealth like a boss. Whether you're looking to boost your bank account or just want to attract more opportunities into your life, Citrine is the crystal for you.

It's like having a little cheerleader in your pocket, cheering you on and helping you reach your goals. Citrine will boost your confidence, clear your mind of limiting beliefs, and help you stay focused on your vision. And if you're someone who struggles with financial insecurity or fear of failure, Citrine will help you see the world through a lens of abundance and prosperity.

Fourth, we have Clear Quartz, the master healer:

Clear Quartz is like the ultimate multitasking crystal. This clear beauty is like a Swiss Army Knife for your spiritual toolbox, and it'll have you feeling like a master healer in no time. Whether you're looking to amplify the energy of other crystals or just want to bring some clarity and balance to your mind, Clear Quartz is the crystal for you.

It's like having a little magical fairy godmother on your side, clearing negativity from your space and bringing in all kinds of positive vibes. Clear Quartz will help you tap into your intuition, enhance your spiritual growth, and promote overall well-being. And if you're someone who struggles with feeling scattered or overwhelmed, Clear Quartz will help you get centred and focused in no time.

So if you're ready to uplevel your spiritual game, don't sleep on Clear Quartz . This clear powerhouse is like a little miracle worker, and it'll have you feeling like a master healer in no time. Trust me, once you try Clear Quartz, you'll wonder how you ever lived without it.

Fifth, we have Black Tourmaline, the ultimate protector.

Black Tourmaline is like a little bodyguard for your soul. This powerful crystal is the ultimate protector, and it'll have you feeling safe and grounded in no time. Whether you're dealing with negative energy or a psychic attack, Black Tourmaline is the crystal for you.

It's like having a little force field around you, blocking out all the bad vibes and keeping you feeling strong and secure. Black Tourmaline will help you stay centred and balanced, even in the midst of chaos and negativity. And if you're someone who struggles with anxiety or feels vulnerable, Black Tourmaline will help you feel empowered and in control.

So if you're ready to take on the world with confidence, don't sleep on Black Tourmaline . This black beauty is like a little warrior princess, protecting you from harm and helping you stand tall. Trust me, once you try Black Tourmaline, you'll wonder how you ever lived without it.

Sixth on our list is Selenite, the angel stone.

Selenite is like a little angel in crystal form. This white beauty is a powerhouse for spiritual growth and enlightenment, and it'll make you feel like you're floating on cloud nine. Whether you're looking to connect with your higher self or tap into your intuition, Selenite is the crystal for you.

It's like having a little bridge to the divine, helping you connect with the universe and all its infinite wisdom. Selenite will help you clear your mind of distractions and tune into your inner voice, so you can make decisions from a place of clarity and wisdom. And if you're someone who feels disconnected or lost, Selenite will help you find your way back to your true self.

So if you're ready to tap into your spiritual side, don't sleep on Selenite . This white powerhouse is like a little magic wand, helping you unlock your full potential and find your place in the universe. Trust me, once you try Selenite, you'll wonder how you ever lived without it.

Last but not least, we have Aventurine, the stone of luck. This green gem will attract good fortune and opportunities into your life, and help you take risks and make bold moves. Feeling lucky? Keep an Aventurine in your pocket, and watch the magic happen.

Aventurine is like a little lucky charm in crystal form. This green gem is the ultimate stone of luck, and it'll make you feel like you can take on the world. Whether you're looking to attract good fortune or take risks and make bold moves, Aventurine is the crystal for you.

It's like having a little rabbit's foot or a four-leaf clover in your pocket, giving you an extra boost of confidence and good vibes. Aventurine will help you stay optimistic and open to new possibilities, so you can seize every opportunity that comes your way. And if you're someone who feels like you're stuck in a rut, Aventurine will help you break free and start living your best life.

So if you're ready to bring a little luck into your life, don't sleep on Aventurine . This green beauty is like a little magic potion, helping you attract all the good things the universe has to offer. Trust me, once you try Aventurine, you'll wonder how you ever lived without it.

So there you have it, my love. The seven most popular crystals and all their amazing properties. Whether you're looking to manifest love, abundance, protection, or spiritual growth, there's a crystal out there for you. Now go forth and sparkle!

WORKING WITH YOUR CRYSTALS:

Activating your crystals is not just a matter of waving a magic wand and saying "Abracadabra!"

First things first, you need to get your crystals all nice and cleansed. No, not with soap and water, silly! You need to purify them with incense. Just make sure you don't accidentally set your house on fire in the process. Safety first!

Once your crystals are cleansed, it's time to give them a little boost of energy. Hold them in your hands, close your eyes, and take a few deep breaths. Visualise a bright, white light surrounding you and your crystals. Imagine that light filling your crystals with powerful, positive energy.

Now, this next part is important: you need to set your intentions. What do you want your crystals to help you with? Do you need more love in your life? Do you want to feel more grounded and centred? Whatever it is, be clear about it in your mind and focus that intention on your crystals.

Taking a crystal bath or bathing with crystals can be a relaxing and healing experience for many people. When you immerse yourself in water infused with crystals, you allow their energy to enter your body through the skin, providing a gentle and soothing effect that can help balance and heal your energy centres.

To prepare a crystal bath, first, you need to choose the right crystals. Some good options include rose quartz for love and emotional healing, amethyst for relaxation and stress relief, and clear quartz for overall balance and clarity. Make sure the crystals you choose are safe to be submerged in water, and avoid using any porous or fragile stones.

Next, you can either place the crystals directly into the bathwater or place them around the edge of the tub. As you soak in the water, you can hold the crystals in your hands, place them on your body, or simply allow them to float around you. Take deep breaths and focus on the sensations of the water and the crystals, allowing their energy to wash over you.

If you prefer to take a bath with your crystals on you, you can place them on various parts of your body, such as your chest, stomach, or forehead, depending on the healing properties of the specific stones you are using. You can also hold the crystals in your hands or place them on a nearby surface within easy reach.

Whichever method you choose, remember to set your intention for the bath or soak. Think about what you want to achieve or what you want the crystals to help you with. This will help you focus your energy and intention, allowing the crystals to work their magic on you.

And there you have it, my crystal-loving friend! With a little bit of cleansing, energizing, and intention-setting, your crystals will be activated and ready to help you manifest your desires. So go forth and sparkle!

MANIFESTING WITH CRYSTALS:

First things first, you gotta choose the right crystals for the job. Each crystal has its own unique energy and properties, so make sure you pick one that aligns with your desires. Need more abundance in your life? Go for citrine. Want to attract love? Rose quartz is your BFF. And if you need a little extra help with your spiritual growth, amethyst has got your back.

Next, you gotta get your manifestation game on point. This means setting clear intentions and visualizing your desires as if they've already come to fruition. Hold your crystal in your hand, close your eyes, and focus on your intention. Feel the energy of the crystal flowing through you, helping to amplify your manifestation powers.

Last but not least, you gotta trust the process, baby! The universe has got your back, and your crystal is just the cherry on top of the manifesting sundae. Keep your crystal close to you, meditate with it, carry it with you throughout the day, and let its energy remind you of your intentions. And before you know it, your desires will become your reality.

Manifesting with crystals is all about choosing the right stones, setting clear intentions, and trusting the process.

CHARGING YOUR CRYSTALS:

Charging your crystals is like giving them a little spa day, so they can release all that negative energy and come back stronger than ever. But you gotta be careful with the sun. Some crystals can't handle all that heat and light, and they'll end up looking like a hot mess. So which crystals should you charge in the sun? Let me break it down for you.

First things first, you gotta choose the right crystals for the job. Some crystals, like Citrine and Amethyst, love basking in the sun's rays, while others, like Rose Quartz and Fluorite, prefer the cool and calming energy of the moon. But there are a few crystals that you should never, and I mean never, charge in the sun. These delicate beauties, like Malachite and Celestite, can be damaged or even destroyed by too much sun exposure.

So, if you're looking to charge your crystals in the sun, make sure you choose the right ones. And remember, it's not just about leaving them out in the sun all day. You gotta set your intentions, and visualise your crystals absorbing all that positive energy from the sun's rays. And if you're feeling extra fancy, you can even use a magnifying glass to focus the sun's energy on your crystals, giving them an extra boost of power.

So go ahead, and give your crystals the spa day they deserve. Charge them up with the energy of the sun, or the calming energy of the moon, and watch as they shine brighter than ever before. Trust me, your crystals will thank you for it.

CHAPTER 12: MOVING TO A NEW EARTH

As I mentioned earlier, one of the most important aspects of the spiritual awakening process is healing, both individually and as a collective. When we heal ourselves, we create a ripple effect of positive change that extends far beyond our own individual experience.

One of the ways in which this healing can manifest is by stopping the patterns of attacking each other and operating from a place of fear and lack. We're all interconnected, and when we attack each other, we're really just attacking ourselves.

By waking up to this truth and learning to operate from a higher vibration of love, compassion, and understanding, we can create a world that operates from a new paradigm. Some people call this the new earth, but whatever you choose to call it, the important thing is that it's a world where we're all connected and supported on our journey.

In this new paradigm, we're no longer operating from a place of scarcity and fear, but from a place of abundance and love. We're no longer competing with each other, but collaborating and supporting each other's growth and healing.

The key to moving into this new paradigm is by living in the present moment and focusing on our own healing and growth. By doing so, we create a positive impact on the world around us and inspire others to do the same.

Through practices like meditation, energy healing, and connecting with higher realms of consciousness, we can tap into the infinite wisdom of the universe and align our thoughts, feelings, and beliefs with what we want to manifest.

As we heal ourselves and one another, we create a world that operates from a higher vibration of love and light. We create a world where we can all thrive and live in harmony with each other and with the Earth.

The New Earth concept believes that it is possible for individuals and humanity as a whole to reach this elevated state of existence through spiritual practice, personal growth, and collective evolution.

Ditching the old duality and moving on to a more loving, heart-based consciousness, it's like being reborn as a Divine Creator.

With each breath, you're writing the script for your very own New Earth adventure. Want in on the action? It's all up to you, my friend. Participation is voluntary, and whether you join the cosmic party or sit this one out, you're still a mighty creator, baby!

And let's not forget our beautiful Mother Earth, aka Gaia, she's evolving too! Can you even imagine our planet as a conscious, living being? We're just little fleas on her back, but she loves us despite all the harm we've done. But that's a story for another day. The choice is yours, join Gaia's ascension to higher vibrations and dimensions, or resist the change

Moving into the New Earth can be a personal journey that involves shifts in one's perspective, beliefs, and ways of being in the world. The New Earth isn't just any old vacation spot, it's a whole new vibe in the 5th dimension. But, only for those who are ready to kick their spiritual growth into overdrive.

Channelling the Arcturians a lot has helped me understand that the goal is to move into a new paradigm, because we've heard this earth so much, that if we don't do something about it soon, on a spiritual level, then it's not going to look good. That's why so many of the galactic beings have been close to the earth, to help us with the Ascension.

The concept of Earth "ascending" can have different meanings depending on the context in which it is used.

In spiritual and metaphysical circles, the idea of Earth ascending refers to a process in which the planet and all its inhabitants are believed to be undergoing a shift in consciousness or a vibrational frequency that leads to a higher level of awareness and spiritual evolution. This process is often referred to as the "Ascension" or the "Great Shift" and is believed to bring about a new era of peace, harmony, and unity among all beings.

If individuals have a multitude of personal issues, they are unlikely to be in a position to assist others. Likewise, if they are incapable of taking care of their own well-being, it may be challenging for them to act in the best interests of the planet.

See, we've made a lot of progress in the tech department, but we've been seriously slacking when it comes to matters of the heart. We've been bulldozing our way through life without taking the time to develop compassion and empathy, and it's been a total disaster.

So here's the deal - we need to get our hearts in check before we go any further. We need to focus on evolving our hearts and aligning them with the knowledge and understanding that we've gained through our technological advancements. 'Cause let's face it, without that heart balance, we're just gonna keep running into the same problems over and over again.

Now, I know what some of you might be thinking - "Oh, but

technology is so cool and shiny! Who needs heart balance when you've got robots and virtual reality?" Well, let me tell ya , those things ain't gonna save us. It's gonna take a whole lotta heart to navigate the challenges that lie ahead.

So let's get to work on evolving our hearts, and making sure that compassion is at the forefront of everything we do. 'Cause at the end of the day, it's our capacity for love and connection that will truly make the difference.

If we don't start by working on healing our hearts, we ain't gonna get nowhere.

I know, I know, it's not as exciting as flying cars and teleportation, but trust me, this is where the real work is at. We've gotta take a good hard look at ourselves and start doing the inner work necessary to heal the wounds and traumas that we've been carrying around for far too long.

'Cause let's be real, how can we expect to create a new world when we're still carrying around all this old baggage? We've gotta do the work to release those old patterns and beliefs, and start showing up as the highest versions of ourselves.

Now, I ain't gonna lie, this work ain't easy. It can be messy, uncomfortable, and downright painful at times. But if we wanna move to a new world, it's gotta start with us. We've gotta be willing to look within and do the work to heal our hearts, so that we can show up as the best versions of ourselves and create a world that reflects that.

So let's roll up our sleeves and get to work, folks. 'Cause if we wanna move to a new world, we've gotta start with the foundation - and that foundation is a healed whole heart.

THE ILLUSION OF SEPARATION:

See, we've been living under this illusion that we're all separate from one another - that we're just a bunch of individuals floating around in our own little bubbles, disconnected from the world around us.

But let me tell ya, that's a load of hogwash. The reality is, we're all interconnected - every single one of us. We're all part of this big, beautiful, messy tapestry called life, and each and every one of us has a role to play in it.

But the truth is, that feeling of separation is just an illusion - a story that we've been telling ourselves for far too long.

The reality is, we're all connected through a web of energy that links us all together. Every thought, every action, every word we speak - it all ripples out and affects the world around us.

So the next time you're feeling alone or disconnected, I want you to remember this: you're never truly alone. You're part of something bigger than yourself - a beautiful, interconnected web of life that links us all together.

The society we live in today tries to convince us that we're all just separate individuals, living our own separate lives, but that couldn't be further from the truth. The reality is, we're all connected - not just on a soul level, like I mentioned before, but also on a material level.

You see, we live in a world that's driven by money and

power. And that system thrives on convincing us that we're all just separate individuals, competing against each other for resources and success. But the truth is, that's just a manipulation tactic - a way to keep us divided and distracted so that we don't realise our true power.

Think about it: if we all realised that we're actually part of a collective whole - that we're all part of the same web of life, and that our actions and choices impact everyone and everything around us - we'd be a force to be reckoned with. We'd be unstoppable in our pursuit of a more just and equitable world.

So don't buy into the fear agenda, my friends. Don't let society convince you that you're just an isolated individual, living in a vacuum. Remember that you're part of something greater than yourself, and that your choices and actions have the power to shape the world around you. Embrace your interconnectedness, and use it to create a future that's more loving, more compassionate, and more connected than we ever thought possible.

So let's ditch the illusion of separation, and embrace the truth of our interconnectedness. 'Cause when we do that, we can start to create a world that truly reflects the love, compassion, and beauty that exists within all of us.

I'm just coming to grips with the idea of interconnectedness myself, and it's a lot to take in. I've been conditioned to believe in the illusion of separation for so long that accepting the truth of it all as day-to-day knowledge is a process.

But the more I channel the Arcturians and Angel Michael and explore the deeper truths of the universe, the more open I become to the idea of interconnectedness. I'm starting to notice subtle shifts in my life - coincidences and synchronicities that I never paid attention to before, and a greater sense of empathy and compassion for the people and world around me.

It's still a challenge to fully accept this truth, but I'm committed to the process. I'm keeping an open mind, exploring new ideas, and incorporating the knowledge of interconnectedness into my daily life. I believe that the more I do this, the more joy, peace, and fulfillment I'll experience in all aspects of my life.

You see, advanced civilisations understand something that we mere mortals often overlook: that we're all part of the same soul, separated into lots of individual souls, but part of a collective group soul.

Think of it like this: you and I might look different, sound different, and even have different beliefs and values. But deep down, we're all connected - we're all part of the same big, beautiful soul that permeates the universe.

And it's not just you and me, either. Every single living being on this planet is part of that same soul - from the tiniest insect to the mightiest elephant, from the grass growing in your backyard to the towering trees of the Amazon rainforest.

The truth is, this understanding of our collective soul is what allows advanced civilizations to evolve beyond petty squabbles and conflicts. They recognise that, at our core, we're all the same - that our differences are just surface-level, and that deep down, we're all part of something greater than ourselves.

So let's take a page from their book, folks. Let's recognise the interconnectedness of all life, and work together to create a world that reflects that truth. 'Cause when we do that, we can tap into the incredible power of our collective soul, and create a future that's more beautiful, more compassionate, and more loving than we ever thought possible.

When we only think of ourselves as individuals, we miss out on the bigger picture of interconnectedness and the impact our actions have on the world around us. This mindset can lead to a lack of empathy and understanding for others, and a disregard for the impact our choices have on the environment and society.

Furthermore, when we only focus on our individual needs and wants, we may become more competitive, selfish, and isolated. This can lead to a lack of collaboration and cooperation, hindering progress and innovation in our personal and professional lives.

In contrast, when we embrace the idea of interconnectedness and acknowledge our role in the larger collective, we open ourselves up to a greater sense of purpose, compassion, and unity. We become more aware of the impact of our actions on others and the world, and strive to make choices that benefit not only ourselves but also those around us.

So, it's important to break free from the limiting belief that we are solely individuals and start recognizing the power of our connections and relationships. By doing so, we can create a more harmonious and fulfilling existence for ourselves and the world around us.

HOW TO HELP GET TO A NEW EARTH:

So, if you're ready to shake things up and elevate your consciousness. Here are some steps that you can take to move towards the New Earth:

Practice self-awareness and self-reflection: Get to know yourself better, and become aware of your thoughts, emotions, and beliefs.

This process can help you identify any limiting beliefs or negative thought patterns that may be holding you back, as well as provide an opportunity to challenge and change them. Additionally, self-reflection can help you gain a greater understanding of your values, strengths, and weaknesses, allowing you to cultivate a greater sense of self-awareness and self-confidence.

To practice self-awareness and self-reflection, you can start by setting aside time each day to meditate, journal, or engage in other mindfulness practices. This quiet time can provide the space you need to reflect on your experiences, thoughts, and feelings, and gain greater insight into your inner world. Additionally, consider engaging in activities that challenge you to step outside of your comfort zone, such as taking a class, traveling, or trying new things. These experiences can help you to grow and develop in new ways, and can provide valuable opportunities for self-reflection and growth.

Finally, it's important to cultivate healthy relationships

with others, and to seek out guidance and support from trusted friends, family members, or a therapist. Talking about your experiences and receiving feedback from others can be incredibly valuable in helping you to gain a deeper understanding of yourself, and can help you to make positive changes in your life.

1. Embrace love and positivity: Cultivate love, gratitude, compassion, and positivity in your life, and let go of negative thoughts and feelings.

It's about taking a step back and examining your thoughts, feelings, and beliefs, and making sure that they align with love and positivity.

One way to do this is by practicing gratitude on a daily basis. Take a moment each day to think about all the things you are thankful for in your life, big or small. This helps shift your focus to the positive things in your life and can have a big impact on your overall mood and well-being.

Another way to embrace love and positivity is to let go of negative thoughts and feelings. This doesn't mean you ignore or suppress negative emotions, but instead, you process and release them in a healthy way. Try to focus on the present moment, and choose to see the good in people and situations.

1. Connect with others: Build meaningful relationships with others, and practice empathy and understanding towards those who are different from you.

When we reach out to others and build relationships based on trust, respect, and empathy, we not only enrich our own lives but also make a positive impact on the lives of others. This connection can be built through small acts of kindness, such as lending a listening ear, sharing a smile, or offering a helping hand.

In order to connect with others, it is important to practice empathy and understanding. This means being open to others' perspectives, experiences, and beliefs, even if they are different from our own. It also means being willing to put ourselves in someone else's shoes and see things from their point of view. This can be a challenging but rewarding practice that can deepen our connections with others and help us to build bridges across differences.

Another way to connect with others is to participate in activities that bring people together. This can be anything from volunteering, joining a sports team, or simply spending time with friends and family. When we connect with others in a meaningful way, we not only build relationships but also foster a sense of belonging and community.

Serve others and the planet: Find ways to give back and contribute to the well-being of others and the planet. Serving others and the planet is a big part of the new earth movement. It's about finding ways to make a positive impact and make the world a better place. This can involve volunteering, donating to charity, or simply being kind to those around you. By giving back, we not only help others, but we also feel fulfilled and connected to something greater than ourselves. Plus, it's a great way to spread love and positivity. Whether it's through a big action or small gestures, every bit counts and can make a difference. So find ways to give back that resonate with you, and make it a regular part of your life. You'll feel the love and positivity ripple out and touch those around you.

Cultivate spiritual growth: Engage in spiritual practices such as meditation, prayer, or mindfulness that help you connect with a higher power and expand your consciousness. It involves engaging in practices and rituals that help you connect with a higher power, expand your consciousness, and find inner peace and fulfillment. These practices can range from meditation, prayer, and mindfulness, to yoga, chanting, and reading spiritual texts. Each person's spiritual journey is unique, and there is no right or wrong way to practice spirituality. The most important thing is to find what resonates with you, and to make it a regular part of your life. Whether you prefer to spend time in solitude, in a group setting, or in nature, the goal is to create a deeper connection with yourself, with others, and with the world around you. When you engage in spiritual growth, you tap into a source of wisdom and love that is always available to you, and you experience a greater sense of purpose, peace, and joy in life.

Release limiting beliefs and patterns: Let go of limiting beliefs and patterns that hold you back, and embrace new perspectives and ways of being.

Releasing limiting beliefs and patterns can be a liberating experience, like freeing yourself from the chains that have kept you from fully living and experiencing the world. These beliefs and patterns often come from past experiences and can shape our thoughts, behaviours, and emotions. But, it's important to recognise that they don't define who we are and we have the power to change them.

It can be helpful to start by becoming aware of these beliefs and patterns and identifying the underlying cause. This might involve some self-reflection and introspection, but it's worth it! Once you've identified them, it's time to challenge them. Ask yourself if they are truly serving you, or if they are holding you back from reaching your full potential.

Next, replace the limiting beliefs and patterns with more empowering ones. This might take some time and effort, but it's important to surround yourself with positivity and love. Surround yourself with people who support and encourage you, and seek out resources that will help you grow and develop.

Finally, practice, practice, practice! New beliefs and patterns take time to form, so be patient and persistent. Celebrate your successes, no matter how small, and keep pushing forward. Remember, you have the power to create the life you want, and by releasing limiting beliefs and patterns, you open yourself up to new possibilities and experiences.

Foster a sense of community: Join communities of like-minded individuals who support each other on the journey towards the New Earth. Being a part of a community where everyone is aligned in their values, beliefs, and goals can be incredibly fulfilling and empowering. When you surround yourself with people who share your vision of creating a better world, you can learn from each other, grow together, and hold each other accountable in a loving and supportive way. This sense of community can help you stay motivated, inspired, and connected, even when the journey gets tough. Whether it's an in-person group, an online forum, or a spiritual organisation, finding a community that resonates with you can be a crucial step in moving towards the New Earth. As you build relationships with others, you'll likely find that you're more likely to stay the course and continue to evolve in a positive direction, knowing that you're not alone on this journey.

These steps can help you move towards the New Earth, but remember that it is a personal journey and may look different for everyone. The most important thing is to stay true to yourself and your own path towards growth and evolution.

A wide range of spiritual teachers, channelers, and researchers who have delved into the topic. Some of these authors include Eckhart Tolle, Esther Hicks, Gregg Braden, Dolores Cannon, David Wilcock, and Drunvalo Melchizedek, among many others.

These authors offer a variety of perspectives and techniques for achieving a higher consciousness and elevating ourselves to the new earth. They often emphasise the importance of personal growth, self-awareness, and connection to the divine, as well as the need for humanity to shift away from fear-based thinking and towards love, compassion, and unity.

Whether through meditation, energy work, spiritual practices, or other means, these authors offer guidance and insights into the path towards a more enlightened existence. By tapping into their wisdom and incorporating their teachings into our lives, we can better understand the new earth and how to navigate the shift towards a more harmonious and sustainable world.

Your spiritual awakening is not just about your personal growth and evolution, but also about your role in contributing to the collective awakening of humanity and the planet. As you become more aware and aligned with the truth of the universe, you are better equipped to help others who are also on their journey of spiritual awakening.

The entire purpose of embarking on a spiritual awakening journey is to awaken to your inner power, heal your past wounds, and step into your highest and best self. This transformative journey requires you to let go of limiting beliefs, negative patterns, and conditioning that may be holding you back from living a fulfilling and purposeful life. It's about tuning into your intuition and aligning with your true purpose, passions, and values. As you heal and grow, you become more in touch with your inner wisdom and strength, and you are better able to navigate life's challenges with grace and resilience. Ultimately, the goal of spiritual awakening is to live a life of authenticity, joy, and inner peace.

Together, we can pave the way towards a new earth, one that is characterised by love, harmony, and unity. By sharing our knowledge, experiences, and insights, we can create a ripple effect that expands the consciousness of humanity as a whole.

But this journey is not always easy. It requires dedication, perseverance, and a willingness to face our fears and limitations. However, the rewards are immense, not just for ourselves, but for the planet as a whole.

Working on your healing journey and connecting with something bigger than yourself is like a one-two punch for your soul. Not only will you benefit from inner peace and joy, but you'll also radiate good vibes that'll make everyone want to get on your level.

Living your best life and showing others how it's done is the ultimate flex, and it might just inspire them to get their own act together. And let's be real, who wouldn't want to be part of a world that's conscious and compassionate? You've got the power to change your life and make the world a better place.

So embrace your spiritual awakening, and use it as a tool to contribute to the shift towards a more enlightened and sustainable world. Together, we can create a brighter future for ourselves, for future generations, and for Gaia herself.

To your awakening, happiness and healing.

Printed in Great Britain
by Amazon

23217038R00175